The Interpretation of Dreams

By
**Prophetess Deborah
Denise Caldwell**

Copyright @2021 by Deborah Caldwell

All rights reserved. No part of this book may be reproduced in any form or by any electronic or mechanical means, including information storage and retrieval systems, without permission in writing from the publisher, except by reviewers, who may quote brief passages in a review.

This publication contains the opinions and ideas of its author. It is intended to provide helpful and informative material on the subjects addressed in the publication. The author and publisher specifically disclaim all responsibility for any liability, loss or risk, personal or otherwise, which is incurred as a consequence, directly or indirectly, of the use and application of any of the contents of this book.

WORKBOOK PRESS LLC
187 E Warm Springs Rd,
Suite B285, Las Vegas, NV 89119, USA

Website:	https://workbookpress.com/
Hotline:	1-888-818-4856
Email:	admin@workbookpress.com

Ordering Information:
Quantity sales. Special discounts are available on quantity purchases by corporations, associations, and others. For details, contact the publisher at the address above.

ISBN-13:	978-1-955459-60-0 (Paperback Version)
	978-1-955459-61-7 (Digital Version)

REV. DATE: 20.05.2021

Acknowledgements

My deepest appreciation to....

All those who encouraged me and labored with me in prayer, project, and financial support to brink this book to completion; to Ellen Murphy a friend and teacher a Faith Family Academy Oak Cliff, to her last year class for their questions which helped me to prepare me for the questions would be asked.

I want to thank my children; Adrian, Shequetta, Roshonda, Crystal, and Sophia; also my grandchildren, Makayla, Josie, Kenterria, but this book would not be complete without the acknowledgement of my late grandson Damascus Wayne Jones for after his death I encountered a closer walk with the Lord.

Most important, my gratitude to my Lord and Savior Jesus for His grace and companionship during this project and the Holy Spirit's faithful guidance through this assignment.

Table of Contents

Chapter 1 Ways God Speaks To Us………………………………..8

Chapter 2 Spiritual Muscles………………………………………..…14

Chapter 3 Dream Interpretations………………………………..23

Chapter 4 Prophecy, Word of Knowledge and Word of Wisdom………………………..…………....……………30

Chapter 5 Dream Symbols……………………………………..34

Chapter 6 God's Government………………………………….…38

Chapter 7 The Hands of God Ministry……………………..42

Chapter 8 More Interpreting Your Dreams…..…………….46

Chapter 9 Faith Connections To Dreams……………………50

Chapter 10 Revelations That John Saw In A Vision……………………………………………….56

Chapter 11 Giftings……………………………….…....………….62

Chapter 12 God's Kingdom……………………………….…....69

Chapter 13 God's Kingdom Covenant ……………………….87

Chapter 14 More Dream Symbols, Faith and Mysteries of the Kingdom……………...…..……………………….78

Chapter 15 Open Heavens………………………………….86

Chapter 16 The Living Word and Stars………………………96

The Interpretation of Dreams
Introduction

One of the ways God speaks to us is through dreams and visions. God speaks to us in many ways and the most primary way is through His Word. Dreams given by the Spirit are no different from prophecy, Word of knowledge, Word of wisdom. Dreams are night visions and these supernatural occurences with God can happen in a dream, in a vision of the night or when deep sleep falls upon you as you are slumbering upon the bed. Dreams are just another way the Lord chooses to speak to His servants at a given time. The Holy Spirit connects and gives you the message that He wants to speak to you about. God sometimes speaks to us when we are in our sleep, because we are so busy during our everyday life with all the noise and distractions. When our body slows down as we sleep, our spirit is open where God can visit and speak to us in a dream or vision.

Chapter 1
Ways God Speaks To Us

These are just a few ways God Speaks to His People

1. Speaks through His Word

2. Speaks Audio voice

3. Still small voice

4. Journaling

5. Dreams

6. Vision

Ways God Speaks To Us

For the weapons of our warfare are not carnal, but mighty through God to the pulling down of strongholds (2nd Corinthians 10:4).

There's power in the Word of God and this occurs when we study, meditate and absorb in our spirits what is written. When we study the Word of God on a daily basis, the Word can wash and cleanse our mind, body and spirit if we allow it to. As we allow the Word to change us from the inside and out, it begins to transform us spiritually and naturally as well. Once the scriptures are ingrained within us, we can live and act like what the Word says as Jesus did. Jesus was the Word of God because He walked and talked the scriptures completely. Just like Jesus, the Word of God should become so much part of us that we live what the Word says in every area of our lives. Everything in this world began with the Word of God. In John 1:1 it says "In the beginning was God, and the Word was with God, and the Word was God. " Christ is the Living Word of God and the scripture is the written word of God. One time, I explained this to a young man who was confused about Jesus being the living Word of God and that once you become born again, that Jesus begins to live on the inside of you. Meaning the living Word of God will be dwelling on the inside of you as well. When you read your bible, you are reading the living Word of God and once this Word gets inside you then you have Jesus dwelling on the inside of you as well. It was like a light switch came on inside the young man when he finally understood what this meant in a spiritual sense. He said," Wow! I never thought or look at it like that." I was so excited and happy for him!

The Word of God continues to do an inner working on the inside of a person once it gets deep down in your spirit. God's Word has an innate spiritual energy that exudes power from God which makes it alive in us. There is life spiritually as well as naturally in God's Word. There is an inner working of the Word that possesses an innate spiritual energy which makes the Word of God truly alive. The Word is a spirit, active and powerful. It is more powerful than a two-edged sword. The Word speaks to our circumstances and problems. God is so awesome in all that He says and does through His Word. Learn to eat, grow, and live by the Word of God. Learn to listen to His voice through His Word as it says in John 10:27,

"My sheep know my voice and a stranger they will not follow" (KJV).

The Word Gives Faith

The Word of God produces faith inside of us as faith cometh by hearing the Word of God (Romans 10:17 KJV). How do you hear? God's Word is proclaimed, the believer hears the Word and then faith develops out of receiving and hearing the Word of God.

The Word gives Light

Gods' Word brings light and revelation to the believer. Psalms 119: 130 states, "The entrance of thy words give light; it gives understanding unto the simple." When God's Word enters our heart, it brings light and understanding. James 1:22 say the Word of God is as a mirror that brings spiritual revelation. When we behold and look into the mirror of the Word by reading and studying, we recognize the kind of person we are before God. God speaks to us through His Written Word. The Word of God is a mirror that reveals positive and negative things in our lives. The Word will speak to our spiritual unclearness and sickness of any kind, but we can find forgiveness, cleansing, and healing. So God speaks to us through His Word even as the messenger gives the message.

The Audio Voice

I remember before I became a believer, I would be asleep in the quiet still of the night hearing this voice outside my body. The still small voice would call my name "Deborah ", loudly but gently. My eyes would open and sometimes I would get up walk around my place where I was living just to see who was calling my name. I thought to myself that it was just my mind playing tricks on me. God was calling me to come to Him, but I went on with my life of rebellion and sin yet I kept hearing this voice time after time. I would think in my mind, 'Lord you know I am angry with you and I don't want to speak with you so surely you not calling me.' Yes, that was my attitude toward God, but in all of my ignorance and blindness, God loved me in spite of being blind by the enemy's deception. Sometimes the enemy blinds us by making us think that God is at fault and does not care about our well-being. This is how he deceived Eve in the book of Genesis.

Genesis 3:1 Now the serpent was more subtle than any beast of the field which the Lord God has made. And he said unto the woman, yea, hath God said, ye shall not eat every tree of the garden? 2. And the woman said unto the serpent, we may eat of the fruit of the trees of the garden. 3. But of the fruit of the tree which is in the mist of the garden, God hath said, ye shall not eat of it neither shall ye touch it least ye die 4. And the serpent said unto the woman, ye shall not surely die: 5. For God does know that in the day you eat thereof, then you eyes will be opened, and you shall be as Gods knowing good and evil."

This was truly warfare against the woman's mind because it started on the outside with the voice of the deceiver and moved to the inside of her mind. This became a battle for Eve's soul by the temptation that the Enemy was bringing to her not knowing what was really going on through deception and lies. We have to be aware of Satan's tactics and schemes knowing that what God say is absolute and there is now compromise or gray areas in obeying His commands unlike Eve who disobeyed suffering the consequences. He is a God that loves with an everlasting love even when we fall short and sin. G o d s a y s i n J e r e m i a h 3 1 : 3 , " I have love thee with an everlasting love threw love and kindness have I drawn thee,"(KJV). Always listen for that voice of truth for it is the voice of our God.

The Still Small Voice

Zechariah 4:6 KJV *Not by might, nor by power, but by my Spirit.* Because of the indwelling of the Holy Spirit, God can now speak to His people through His Spirit. The still small gentle voice of God speaks to us individually and personally. In The Old Testament, God spoke to His prophets in dreams and visions. God can speak to us while we are in a peaceful sleep. God's promptings and leadings start in your spirit man from the Holy Spirit when Jesus told His disciples that he must go away in order for the Holy Spirit to come. John 16:7 "But I tell you the truth; it is to your advantage that I go away, for if I do not go away the helper will not come to you, but if I go I will send him to you. 8. And he when he comes will convict the world of sin and righteousness and Judgment".

He Will Lead and Guide you into all Truth

John 16:13 "Howbeit when he, the spirit of truth is come he will guide you into all truth; for he shall not speak of himself; but whatsoever he shall hear, that shall he speak; and he will show you thing to some. 14. He shall glorify me: for he shall receive of mine, and shall show it unto us. 15. All things that the father hath are mine: therefore, said I that he shall take have mine, and shall show it unto you." (KJV).

His still small voice, that prompting in your spirit that speaks to our heart to gently leading and guiding us into the things of God. He is there to inspire, reveal, and encourage the things you would have not known or seen on your own. That still small voice will keep us on the straight and narrow. The more time we spend with God by reading His Word, praying, and worshiping Him, the clearly we hear His voice and learn to obey Him. It says in Isaiah 1: 1 that," If you will be willing, and obedient you shall eat the good of the land" (KJV). I have heard that still small voice speaks those exact words to me. There is a prompting in our spirit, and you know that is the voice from God through his Holy Spirit. It is like nothing you have heard before. God speaks to us but He may speak to you differently from the way He speaks to me but He has a way of using what you are familiar with to communicate with you. These are ways God speaks to me and probably you as well. I hope and pray this will help you to understand how He communicates with you, but out of it all God gets the glory. Listen to the promptings of the

Holy Spirit for He is a gentleman whose voice speaks to our hearts. It is that personal communion with him and God that we can listen to God clearly and intently. Let Him teach you to hear His voice. God wants to communicate with you.

I love the way He speaks to me and you will too, but you may have to travail much in prayer, fasting, and whatever it takes to get to know Him and hear Him speak to you. It will be well worth hearing from God, our creator, who has created the world and universe. Right now I am on a journey for my purpose and destiny for existing in the earth at this current time. Yes, we all have a purpose and destiny preordained by God. I am so excited about this journey and so should you. God will speak but however He speaks, we must be very attentive to His still small voice. God is such awesome and glorious being to have a relationship with as we look in the book of 1st Kings 19:12-13 in which it reads, "And after the earthquake a fire; but the Lord was not in the fire; and after the fire a still small voice, so it was when Elijah heard it, that he wrapped his face in his mantle, and went out, and stood in the entrance of cave, and behold, there came a voice unto him, and said, what are you doing here, Elijah?" (KJV). In His still small voice in which there was no visible display of power, God was still at work. Thus like the silent morning light, grace works upon man. Its process is owed by Love and there is a touch of terror or bondage in the great reconciling deed within the gospel with its gold tidings as it leaps out to reveal the heart of God as it enters the heart of men. The rest follows with sacred gratitude as God devour his enemies with lions and rescues His friends but He wins all the time in the end. God wins with love with those that are unyielding as He break with a rod of iron dashing them into pieces like potter's vessels, but for His own making. When He comes to save them, He touches them with the silver scepter of mercy as grace works the oiled feather. The still small voice of God will saturate your heart in a time of need. Just open your heart and listen.

Chapter 2

Spiritual Muscles

Prayer is another way God speaks when we take prayer seriously, and learn to pray as Jesus did then God begins to become real to us in our lives and answer our prayers. I had a prayer partner for years. We would pray every morning and everyday at 6:00 a.m. we called as we ourselves intercessors and prayer warriors. We would pray and cry out to God everyday so we thought. We weren't sure if our prayers were being heard but we wanted to be the women who prayed for ourselves, families, friends, communities, government, our finances, churches, saved, and unsaved. We called ourselves "Wailing Women at the Well" but little did we know that we were not following the pattern of prayer that Jesus taught in the book of Matthew 6:6 in which Jesus said, "when you pray, go into your closet in secret and pray and your Father who see you in secret will reward you openly" (KJV). Sometimes we would get lucky in prayer and some prayers were not being answered but for the most part we were going through the motions. The issues and circumstances were overwhelming in our lives with my prayer partner having problems with her marriage, and me having problems with my grandson. Every morning we would pray, pray, and pray.

A Form of Prayer

On February 22, 2013 I received a phone call that my grandson Damascus Jones was shot. I grab my car keys on my way to the hospital to help my grandson not knowing what happen, or who was responsible for the tragic of my grandson. I was greeted by the attending Doctor who said, "Damascus lost a lot of blood and we are doing all we can to save him". I called me pray partner numerous of time, but she never answered my calls. Now reality was setting in. I needed someone to help me stand in the gap for him and help me pray through his life was in my hands a matter of life and death. It was so much distractions in the hospital that now everybody was there. Who would pray with me? Who would understand that we have to get an emergency prayer through? I was tired, but to no avail could I get anyone to pray with me. I was disappointed even with myself. We lost him about 3:00 a.m. in the morning and surely God had been listening to our prayers. Then, I heard the Lord say to me, "A form of godliness." "What?" Was my response to God a form of Godliness? I felt like the Patriarch Job.

> *Job 1: 13- 22 (ESV) Now there was a day when his sons and daughters were eating and drinking wine in their oldest brothers' house. 14. And a messenger came to Job and said, "The oxen were plowing and the donkeys feeding beside them, 15. When the Sabena's raided them and took them away-indeed. They have killed the servants with edge of the sword; and alone have escaped to tell you." While he was still speaking, another fell from heaven and burned up the sheep and the servants, and consumed them; and I alone have escaped to tell you. 17. While he was still speaking, another also came and said, "the Chaldeans from three bands raided the camels and took the away, yes, and killed the servants with the edge of the sword; and I alone have escaped to tell you!"18. While he was speaking still, another also came and said, "Your sons and daughter were eating and drinking wine in their oldest brothers' house, 19. And suddenly a great wind came from across the wilderness and stuck the four corners of the house, and it fell on the young people, and they are dead; and I alone have escaped to tell you!" 20. Then Job arose, tore his robe, and shaved his head; and he fell to the ground and worship. 21. And*

said, "Naked I came from my mothers' womb, and naked shall I return there the Lord gives, and the Lord has taken 22. All that happened Job did not sin nor charge God with wrong.

Job was a praying man who prayed for his children and his family, but the day came when he had to face something that was not being rightly done in his life and this was a time of testing. When I lost my only grandson of seventeen years after seeing him every day of my life, everything had changed and took a new twist. Now God really had my attention and through this life circumstance, He was teaching me the true meaning of a prayer life. This prayer life did not involve nobody else but me and God. You too can get into a life-changing prayer time with God. A personal one on one prayer time with God will help us learn how to spend time alone with God as He speaks to us through prayer.

These are some of the ways on how God can speak to His Creation. God speaks in so many ways that we must not limit Him to one way for He is God. If you long to hear God speak, don't expect Him to speak to you in a loud voice or in the same manner. God chooses to speak to you how He wants to speak and our part is to learn how He chooses to speak. If you are a dreamer, you can rest assure that He is speaking to you in night visions which are pictures and images that are like a movie or watching something on television. Get it, Tel-e-vision! There are other ways He speaks to His People such as through our circumstances, our praise and worship time. Find the vein that God is speaking to you because sometimes we can't explain what happens in our life and don't understand what's going on. We need to pay close attention what He is saying to you. God is mysterious in His own way, but He has created each of us in His Own Image to make sure we can discern what is God and not some other spirit. God will allow things to happen in our life not because He is being mean or harsh, but to get our attention and to draw you closer to Him to keep you in His Will or bring you back into His Will for your life. The things that happen in our life can either bring us closer to God, Our Creator or push us farther away from Him so we can blame God for all of our misfortune. Or we can simply just surrender and say, "Here I am Lord. I surrender. What do you want me to do or what purpose am I here?" It's all up to you to give Him back what He has given to you to help a lost and dying world.

Christ teaches us how to pray

Matthew 6:5-13 (KJV) And when you pray you shall not be as the hypocrites are: for they love to pray standing in the synagogues and in the corners of the streets, that they may be seen of men. Verily I say unto you, they have their reward. But you, when you pray, enter into your closet, and when thou hast shut you door, pray to you Father which is in secret; and your Father which see in secret shall reward you openly. But when you pray, use not vain repetitions, as the heathen do: for they think that they shall be heard for their much speaking. Be not you therefore like unto them: For your Father know what things you have need of, before you ask him.

After this manner therefore pray you: Our Father which art in heaven, Hallowed be thy name. Thy kingdom come, Thy will be done in earth, as it is in heaven. Give us this day our daily bread. And forgive us our debts, as we forgive our debtors. And lead us not into temptation, but deliver us from evil: For yours are the kingdom, and the power, and the glory, forever. Amen.

The Secret Place

Matthew 6:5-12 (KJV) He that dwells in the secret place of the most high shall abide under the shadow of the all mighty. I will say of the Lord, he is my refuge and my fortress: My God, in him will I trust. Surely he shall deliver me from the snare of the fowler, and from the noisome pestilence. He shall cover me with his feathers, and under his wings shall thou trust: his truth shall be your shield and buckler. You shall not be afraid for the terror by night; or for the arrow that fly by day. Nor for the pestilence that walk in darkness; nor the destruction that waste at noon day. A thousand shall fall at your right hand, but it shall not come near you. Only with your eyes shall you behold and see the reward of the wicked. Because you have made the LORD, which is my refuge, even the most High, your habitation; there shall any plague come nigh your dwelling. For he shall give his angels charge over you, to keep you in all his ways They shall bear thee up in their hands, least you dash your foot against a stone. You shall tread upon the lion and adder: the young lion and the dragon shall you trample under feet. Because he has set his love upon me, therefore will I deliver him: I will set him on high, because he has known my name? He shall call upon me, and I will answer him: I will be with him in trouble; I will deliver him, and honor him. With long life will I satisfy him, and show him my salvation.

Psalms91:1-16
If we dwell in his secret place, we will be safe--------
Amen

I do not claim to know everything about dreams and interpretations. I am only sharing what I do know and to me it still seems like it is not enough, but we can get so much knowledge where we can also get puffed up with knowledge. The reason I learn to study is that I do not want to be deceived by man like the blind leading the blind. I refuse to be cheated out of my inheritance in this life from not understanding the Word of God for myself. I grew up poor and probably will just getting by when I leave this world, but if I am called to expose truth while I am here then I want to do what I was purpose to do here before I leave. I don't know about anyone else but I want to hear, "Well done you good and faithful servant." I have not always been in this place so I want to take advantage of this place in God. I don't claim to know everything, but that I have learned through experience in my spiritual journey that I am pleased to share with those who will. This book is not for everyone but just a select few. If it does not agree with you, I will not be offended. If this book is for you then I say welcome to the Mystery of the Kingdom as I was led to write. I say to my critics that one day you will get your turn too. If you don't know my struggle and my pain, then you won't understand my praise for that is what we were born

What is Potential?

In the words of the late Mr. Myles Monroe who died in an airplane crash in November 29, 2014.

"Potential is unexposed ability reserved power untapped strength uncapped capabilities unused success ** dormant gifts**hidden talents **latent power."

*Mr. Monroe goes on to say potential is "what you can do that haven't been done** Where you can go that you haven't yet gone** who you can be that you haven't yet been ** what you can imagine that you haven't imagined** how far you can reach that you haven't reached. What you can see that you haven't yet seen** what you can accomplish that you haven't yet accomplished?*

We must stand in the light so that the light will shine in the darkness so the God of Creation can get the Glory in our lives by being made in His image. In order to break generational curses, we must expose and uncover what is on the inside. We have in these bodies treasures in earthly vessels but we must take the time to trace in our own bloodline any generational curses that is hindering the Glory of God being revealed in our lives. God will speak to you in dreams and visions concerning who your ancestors and what curses and spirits are connected to your family lineage. Because of the Blood of Jesus, God allows us to uncover the Mysteries of the Kingdom through dreams, visions and the Word of God. In these last days we need to know God like never before and hear Him in many ways because people aren't reading or don't have time to read their bible. ways we have never known him before people will not or don't have time to read their bible. So if God speaks to you in dreams and visions, I would pay close attention to your dreams because they can be used for good for guidance, direction, and giving a warning that can be live and also applied just like the Word to your everyday life. Yet, dreams and visions has to be tested against the Word of God or it can become a form of witchcraft or sorcery. Sounds crazy doesn't it but very serious and true! Not effectively interpreting dreams can open up another spiritual world that can become demonic in nature so everything including dreams has to be tested by the Word of God. Also, prayer and asking God to interpret dreams helps as well because after all He is the creator of dreams and visions. I love the healing and cleansing dreams because they are the most awesome and refreshing kind of dreams. The garbage kind of dreams helps push out a lot of garbage we picked up over the course of our lives such as superstitions and old wives tales.

Example: if a black cat crosses you that means you're going to have bad luck or if someone sweep your feet with a broom then you will go to jail. This is all garbage, myths, and straight out lies which is why I like dreams that cleanse the soul, mind, brain and the head. Sometimes, we can be so negative because of the environment we live in and expose to on a daily basis which can be purged and purify through our dreams.

Spiritual Muscles

If we are to be effective in the ministry in which we have been called to then must continually grow in Christ and must have a process, practice or a person in our lives that fulfills the function of an apostle, prophet, evangelist, pastor and teacher. The work of the ministry has been lost for so many years, but I think God is restoring this work back to the church. I believe there were only twelve apostles and they walked and talked with Jesus, but I do believe the gifts as spoken in Ephesians are gifts as He gave gifts to men. I believe the body of Christ can operate in these gifts with Christ being the head for we are the body of Christ. Of course there will also be a leadership function in place within the body of Christ to help govern these gifts to make sure they are used in decency and in order. In Ephesians 4:11-16 (KJV), it discusses these gifts were given for the equipping of the saints (people) for the work of the ministry, for the building up of the body which I call spiritual muscles until we all come to the unity of the faith and the knowledge of the Son of God. To maturity and to the measure of the full stature of Christ, we must no longer be children, tossed to and fro and blown about by every wind of doctrine, by people's trickery, by their craftiness in deceitful scheming, but speaking the truth in love. We must be moving up and upward in every way into Him who is the head unto Christ from whom the whole body, joined and knit together by every ligament with which it is equipped, as each part is working properly, promoting the body's growth in building itself up in love. This is how the body of Christ is supposed to function, but we can stay on track by operating our spiritual muscles to fulfill the mission which is to win the lost and revive the body of Christ

The Work of an Evangelist

What It Is

1. To preach the word of God.

2. To instruct the brethren of their responsibilities.

3. To reprove those that sin.

4. To set in order things needed.

5. Training teachers, equipping saints for ministry

6. Teaching against false teachers and false doctrine

7. To set example for brethren, in word and in conduct, in love and in faith

These are all I could find under spiritual muscles as we are to evangelize in the body in the kingdom and be changed in order to help others change. If we are going to church, just have a form of Godliness without change then we are not building up the kingdom we are just here occupying space. One of the reasons I was inspired and motivated to write this book and write my book, The Interpretations of Dreams was because of so much rejection I experienced in my life and ministry. When one is rejected and thrown out as an outcast with a lot of time on their hands to walk alone then they have the choice to do good or evil but I chose to walk with God. When rejection becomes like a companion in your life then you resort to some type of activity which mines became writing. Writing became a Central theme and part of my daily life. I would spend majority of time along as I wrote what I heard from the Lord. I believe this book is for someone to know that rejection is not a bad thing and that if you are a believer and accepted Jesus Christ as your Lord and Saviour, He will never reject you.

Chapter 3
Dream Interpretations

Dreams Are Night Visions
In a Dream, in a vision of the night when deep sleep falls upon men in slumbering upon the bed. Job 33:15 (KJV)

Dreams given by the Spirit and are no different from (Prophecy), Vision, Word of Knowledge, word of Wisdom, given by the congregation under the power of the anointing of the Holy Spirit. Dreams are just another way the Lord chooses to speak to His people at a given time. The Spirit of God gives the message He likes to speak to you about in a dream. Unbelievers have dreams as well, but the difference is the believer has the indwelling of the Holy Spirit. A believer is able to have prophetic dreams where the unbeliever can't have a prophetic dreams, nor able to get wisdom and knowledge because the unbeliever spirit is (dead) not alive. A believer's spirit has been recreated with Christ therefore the believer can commune or communicate with God as in 1st Corinthians 12:11 where the scripture reads, "The gift of the Spirit is as the spirit wills through you."

Category of Dreams

A. Healing Dreams

B. Cleansing Dreams

C. Garbage Dreams

D. Prophetic Dreams

E. Internal Dreams

Healing Dreams

Healing dreams take place in your emotions where circumstances in your life that you faced through life events such as: hurts, pain, rejection, unforgiveness and etc. These dreams are when you were gripped in fear with no interpretations because something has been changed within you because of God healing you from fear, rejection, pain as you begin to change from within. I have had many healing dreams for my pains that were deep within. As a little child, I started out with a mother and daddy up until I was ten years old. My mother and dad separated when they divorced. I was a daddy's girl and loved them both, but I wanted the love and acceptance of my dad. I would do anything to get my dads' love and attention. This break-up took a deep effect within me. I really did not know how much it affected me as a child, but God did some deep healing within me in my adulthood. God is still healing me from past pain and the healing is a process which is one of the reasons God visit us in dreams. God heals however He chooses to heal you according to His will which shall be done in your life. You could dream of someone in your past who hurt you but know that God is healing you of that pain. These healing dreams really help me even though I did not fully understand what I was experiencing as a Dreamer. Rejoice when God is healing you of your past hurts because the Lord is saying that, "I brought healing in your life and its time to let it go."

Cleansing Dreams

According to a dream interpreter, these dreams are the dreams that you live out living out your fantasy, such as seeing yourself preach, speaking at a function, or someone giving you a large amount of money.

Cleansing dreams are temptation, anger, losing control of yourself maybe that day or maybe long time ago. It is a dream of what you desire to do during the day, but held back. Cleansing gives you a release from your emotions and the release you needed from all the stuff build-up inside of you. In this dream; God is cleansing you from all of that emotional build –up from within. You will wake up feeling so good and refreshed. You may even dream of flying or doing something out of the ordinary.

Dream Interpretations

Garbage Dreams as dreams where you put out all the garbage in your life. Reading the Word of God or being exposed to the teaching of the Word by filling your mind with the mind of Christ can help get rid of negative emotions and mindsets. As it reads in Romans 12:1 "Be transform by the renewing of your mind" is vital because our mind is where the battle begins as we intake so much garbage even from our child hood into our adulthood. We all have these dreams, believers and un-believers. Understanding and getting knowledge of these dreams and their category is the key to a successful dreamer. In all thy getting; get an understanding. If these dreams begin to come regular like every time you are asleep and you can't remember what you dream; then these dreams fall into the category of garbage. The dreams purge out all of the bad junk like traditions, religion, old wives' tales, the lies that we have learn over the years that are not true. On a regular basic, these dreams will come.

Prophetic Dreams

God speaks a message to your spirit for direction, guidance, warning, and insight for the believer's spiritual walk. A prophetic dream consists of dreaming internally in which this dream is about you and your current condition with the Lord concerning your ministry, your relationship with Him, and where you stand in ministry with Him. Now don't get confused and discouraged by the word ministry, because we all have a ministry. Our children are our ministry and our husband and wives are our ministry. The word 'ministry' comes from the Greek word meaning to serve. Your job or career can be your ministry. Internal dreams are about you so the symbols might be confusing. If you dream about your child, that is your ministry. That child is a part of your character or maybe your sister or brother is part of your character as every character in your life relates to you. This is called an internal dream and the message is about you. How about dreaming you are pregnant in a dream can mean new birth or something being birth in your life. in your life. Losing the baby or can't find the baby can mean your gift is dying or you're losing something. You are the main character in these dreams. It could be a business, job, career, or gift. Dreams are symbolic dreams that paint a picture. God uses what we are familiar with like family, friends, and job in these types of dreams.

Internal Dreams

Internal Dreams are dreams about you and your current condition with the Lord. These dreams consist of your ministry, your relationship with the Lord, where you are in ministry, and where you are spiritually. The Symbols, Characters are all part of you the mind, will, emotion, spirit and flesh relates to you in these internal dreams. Internal Dreams the message God speaks is about you and for you from his Spirit. You are the main character these dreams seem so real you can't forget about the dream when you awake. These are what you call internal dreams.

Internal Prophetic Dreams

Internal Prophetic Dreams are prophecy, word of knowledge, and word of wisdom dreams in which God is speaking in the past, present, and future. He also speaks of warning and directions of what is going to happen in the future. These dreams consist of knowledge, wisdom and understanding.

1. **Knowledge** –The fear of the Lord is the beginning of knowledge Proverb 1&7 2. Wisdom- The fear of the Lord is the beginning of wisdom Proverbs 9:10

3. **Understanding**-Trust in the Lord with all your heart and lean not unto your own understanding acknowledge him in all thy ways and he shall direct thy path Proverb 3:5-6

This might be a hard lesson to learn but we need all of the above in order to know how and what God is speaking to us in dreams. I have been studying on dreams and vision now for almost four years now for this is one of my passions. As He helps me, I can help others as well. We are seeking the mystery of the kingdom of God through dreams, visions, and the word. Have you ever heard the phrase "God works in mysterious ways?" Well that is a true saying because we do see God in the natural when something happens beyond our natural understanding. That is when we can say, He works in mysterious ways. Dreams and visions are mysterious don't you agree? Interpreting dreams are mysterious and all in the Old Testament of the bible, men and women of faith did not have a bible to read so God would visit them in dreams and visions. They understood what the dream or message was from God.

Joseph's Two Dreams

Genesis 37: 1-11 (KJV) And Jacob dwelt in the land wherein his father was a stranger, in the land of Canaan. These are the generations of Jacob. Joseph, being seventeen years old, was feeding the flock with his brothers; and the lad was with the sons of Belial and with the sons of Zilpah his father's wives: and Joseph brought unto his father their evil report. Now Israel (who was Jacob) God changed his name. He loved Joseph more than all his children, because he was the son of his old age: and he made him a coat of many colors. And when his brothers saw that their father love Joseph more than all his children they hated him and could not speak peaceably unto him. And Joseph (dreamed) a dream and he told it to his brothers: and they hated him more. And he said unto them, Hear, I pray you, this dream which I have dreamed. For, behold we were binding sheaves in the field, and lo my sheaf arose, and also stood upright; and behold your sheaves stood roundabout and made obeisance to my sheaf, and his brothers said to him, shall thou indeed have dominion over us? And they hated him yet more for his dream and for his words. And he dreams yet another dream, and told it to his brothers and said, Behold I have dream a dream more; and, behold the sun and the moon and the eleven stars made obeisance to me. And he told it to his father, and to his brothers: And his father rebuked him, and said unto him, what is this dream that thou has dream? Shall I and thy mother and your brothers indeed come to bow down ourselves to thee to the earth? And his brothers envied him; but his father observed the saying.

The old patriarch knew all about dreams and visions including how to interpret them. We now can learn these parables from the bible and apply them to our everyday practical life. This is the will of God for our life and that He helps me know and learn the Mystery of the Kingdom through dreams, visions, and the Word.

I will now explain the difference between dreams and visions: Dreams are when we are asleep with most dreams done in the early morning between 4a.m. and 5a.m, but we are dreaming all the time day and night however God can visit anytime. The difference between dreams and visions; visions are when we are not sleep but wide awake but you might see a picture flash before your eyes. Some are short and some are longer, but this is different. Let's take a look at the Prophet Isaiah's vision to get a little bit more understanding and insight on visions.

Isaiah's Vision of God

In the year that King Uzziah died I saw also the Lord sitting upon a throne, high and lifted up, and his train filled the temple. Above it stood the seraphims each one had six wings; with two he covered his face, and with two he covered his feet, and with two he did fly, And one cried unto another and said, Holy, Holy, Holy, is the Lord of host; the whole earth is full of his glory. And the post of the door moved at the voice of him that cried, and the house was filled with smoke. Isaiah 6:1-4 (KJV)

I have more dreams than I do visions, but I have visions too where a picture will flash across my eyes like a movie picture. It flashes and go blank. These are considered visions. It is good to have them, but just know that God still speaks through dreams and visions but the interpretation is the hard part.

Chapter 4

Prophecy, Word of Knowledge, and Word of Wisdom

Prophecy

The word or gift of prophecy can be sum up in one word, prediction. The prophets predicted the coming of Jesus Christ and also the prediction of the virgin birth of Christ. Today this gift has been given to the body of Christ for the building up or edifying of the people. In our interpretations of dreams, this is one of the gifts that are exercised in the interpreting of the dreams. It speaks of the past, present and the future. It is a message that God wants to give concerning His will for your life or our spiritual condition or state with Him. Prophecy plays an important part in the interpretations of dreams.

> *Joel 2: 28, Acts 2: 2-14 (KJV) And it will be in the last days I will pour out my spirit on all humanity; then your sons and daughters shall prophesy, you young men will see visions, and you old men shall dream dreams. I will even pour out my spirit on male and female slaves in those days, and they shall prophesy.*

Word of Knowledge

This gift is about knowing the knowledge or the revelation of Christ. We should all grow up in spiritual knowledge of Him and learn of Him. It is like reading people thoughts concerning what they dream as you read the words or listen to their dreams. In this revelation, it is revealed to the one who is helping interpret the dream. It is hidden knowledge from the dreamer that is revealed. It is information given at an appointed time. This gift also has a supernatural capacity to recall or know scriptures related to the dream.

> *Colosians2:1-8 (KJV)For I want you to know how great a struggle in Laodicea, and for all who have not seen me in person. I want their hearts to be encouraged and joined together in love, so that they may have all the riches of assured understanding, and have the knowledge of Gods' mystery—Christ in him all the treasures of wisdom and knowledge are hidden. I am saying this so that no one will deceive you with persuasive arguments. For I may be absent in body, but I am with you in spirit, rejoicing to see you good order and the strength of your faith in Christ. Therefore, as you have received Christ Jesus the Lord, walk in him, rooted and built up in him and established in the faith, just as you were taught, and overflowing with thankfulness. Be careful that no one takes you capacitive through philosophy and empty deceit based on human tradition, based on the elemental forces of the world, and not based on Christ. These gifts work together and some have the gift and don't know it.*

The Gift of Wisdom

The gift of wisdom is different from the gift of knowledge for it is used to apply truth and wisdom understands truth. In dream interpretations, these two must work together. Proverb is a book full of wisdom. These gifts were so profound and used in the Book of Acts even when the bible had not yet been completed. All gifts are to be compared with scriptures. These are to be in line with the Word of God and not outside of His word. All should be in order, line upon line and precept upon precept. It is important that these gifts are in operation with interpreting dreams and visions in the people lives. We can get into error if we don't operate effectively in the interpretation things like giving wrong information when telling someone that God want them to marry or marry a certain person they dream about. We have to study interpretations of dreams just as we have to study all things. The kingdom of God is a mystery only God can and will reveal to us. We will not know or learn everything here, but it is good to know that God is for us and not against us. In all we do, we have to have a prayer life unto God and we have to stay connected to Him. Without Him, we can do little. God speaks through dreams and visions for we have always heard that He speaks through the Word and speaks to us in night visions. This has become my passion to get this out so all who need this revelation is revealed to them so that the Word goes into the heart of the people so we all can understand and know that God speaks not only to a select few. My prayer is that your eyes be open to the truth of what you have been dreaming and come into manifestation by the Word of God.

> *Ephesians 1:15-19 (KJV) Wherefore I also , after I heard of your faith in the Lord Jesus , and love unto all the saints, Ceases not to give thanks for you, making mention of you in my prayers; That the God of our Lord Jesus Christ , the Father of glory , may give unto you the spirit of wisdom and revelation in the knowledge of him: The eyes of your understanding being enlightened ; that ye may know what is the hope of his calling, and what the riches of the glory of his inheritance in the saints, And what is the exceeding greatness of his power to us who believe , according to the working of his might power.*

Category of Dreams

A. Healing Dreams

B. Cleansing Dreams

C. Garbage Dreams

D. Prophetic Dreams

E. Internal Dreams

Chapter 5

Dream Symbols

Interpreting dreams and visions symbols have meaning such as the numbers, the colors, and the places. They all have meanings and this is the part that we apply. We do have the ability to study our dreams and study the symbols associated with our dreams.

> **Numbers 12:6 (KJV) And he said, Hear now my words: If there be a prophet among you, I will make myself known unto him in vision, and will speak in a dream.**

A. **Lamp**: **(Direction)** "Thy word is a lamp to my feet and a light to my path" Psalms 119:105(KJV)

B. **Hammer:** "Is not my word like fire said the Lord like a hammer that break the rock" Jeremiah 23:29 (KJV)

C. **Mirror**: "If any be a hearer of the word, and not a doer, she is like unto a man beholding himself in the mirror" James 1:23-24 (KJV)

D. **Sword:** "For the word of God is alive, active sharper than a two-edge sword" Hebrew 4:12 (KJV)

E. **Seed**: "The seed is the word of God when sown on good ground (the heart) the seed will grow. "Matthew 13:18(KJV)

F. **Hand**: healing or doing war- "Blessed be the Lord is my strength he trains my hands to war" Psalm 144:1 (KJV)

G. **Baby**: new beginning, ministry, new career, new job, business.

H. **Elevator**: -going upward, going down going the wrong way.

I. **Cattle**: prosperity "He owns some cattle on a thousand hill" Psalm 50:10 (KJV)

J. **Hallway**: transitioning

K. **Bathroom**: cleansing, clean a place of repentance.

L. **House**: a person life; what is going on inside Matthew 7

M. **Basement**: hidden thing hidden sin, repress emotions.

N. **Attic**: things from the past.

O. **Kitchen**: a place of devotion, preparing meals.

P. **Living room**: Social life.

Q. **Closet**: A place of prayer.

R. **Home town**: A person past life.

S. **Car**: Ministry.

T. **Bridge**: transition something being delayed.

U. **Bedroom**: A place of intimacy.

V. **Cross Road**: Decision making

W. **Stop sign**: warning, stop, something is ahead.

X. **Rough Road Ahead**: a trial is coming.

Y. **Wrong way**: danger, turn around, start the right thing.

Z. **U-turn**: No turning back.

Dream Symbols of Numbers

1. **One**- beginning, unity
2. **Two**- confirmation – let every word be establish by two or three, witness
3. **Three**- Trinity –Father Son Holy Spirit.
4. **Four**- four seasons, four corners of the earth, worldwide, universal.
5. **Five**- grace, power fivefold ministry.

6. **Six**- the # of man, created on the six day, humanity.

7. **Seven**- number of perfection God rest on the seven day. Day of completion.

8. **Eight**- New beginning starts over.

9. **Nine**- The gifts of the Spirit, the fruits of the Spirit.

10. **Ten** – The Ten Commandments, the number of God's Law and righteousness.

11. **Eleven**-Blessings of double potion

12. **Twelve**- Government, the twelve tribes of Judah authority and dominion.

Colors in Dreams

A. **Red** – the Blood of Jesus Anointing, power, wisdom for battle.

B. **Blue**- Revelation, insight, authority, communion

C. **Purple**- Royalty, Kingship, Priesthood- judges 8:26

D. **White**- Clean, Pure, Righteousness, Holy Angels.

E. **Green**- Prosperity, Growth.

F. **Black**- Mysterious, Death, unknown, Spiritual Darkness.

G. **Yellow**- Hope, Faith, Strength, Gifts from God.

H. **Orange**- The color of fire and autumn leaves perseverance.

I. **Pink**- child-like love of faith- negative immature, childless.

J. **Gray**- Maturity, honor,

K. **Silver**- Redemption will result from this, the price of redeeming.

L. **Brown**-Humility, compassion, pastoral color.

M. **Gold**- Purity, holiness, glory prosperity.

These are just a few symbols as I have studied them learning to interpret dreams is an on-going learning experience in our journey here in the earth. Our heavenly father is eager for us to know him and pursue him to learn the mystery of the kingdom. God is always speaking to us we have to listen and find out how he speaks to us. My prayer is that you find the method God use to speak to you and that you begin a relationship with him for God is not the problem we are our own worst enemy when we do not pursue him. If you don't know Jesus as your personal savior who is the only way to the father then I invite you to ask him into your heart to know him and to have fellowship with him so that you may know your purpose for being born, you calling, quest, you mission. He will come in and sup with you. If you are in religion he will bring you out for he come to save that witch was lost, he come to set the captives free, he come that you may have eternal life and be with him forever. Amen

Chapter 6

God's Government

Unto us a Child is born; unto us a son is given and the government shall be upon his shoulders: and his name shall be called Wonderful, Counselor, the mighty God, The everlasting father, The Prince of Peace. Isaiah 9:6 KJV

In studying God's government in God's Kingdom, these are the things that were given to the Body of Christ which I believe were lost and God is restoring them back to His people. I ask the Lord, "If your government is different from the world government then, what is your government?" Well I did not get an answer right then, but after much studying and search into the scriptures; to my surprise the answers were staring us in the face the whole time. God's government is His gifts and fruits in the kingdom. We are told to seek first the Kingdom of God and his righteousness and all these things shall be added unto us (Matthew 6:33).

Colors in Dreams

1. The Gifts of the Spirit: 1 Corinthians 12: 4-12
Now there are diversities of gifts, but the same Spirit. And there are diversities of operations, but it is the same God which works all in all. But the manifestation of the Spirit is given to every man to profit withal. For to one is given the Spirit of wisdom; to another the word of knowledge by the same Spirit; To another faith by the same Spirit; to another the gifts of healing by the same Spirit; To another the working of miracles; to another prophecy; to another discerning of spirits, to another divers kind of tongues; to another the interpretations of tongues: But all these work that one and selfsame Spirit, dividing to every ma severally as he will. For as the body is one, and hath many

members, and all the members of that one body, being many, is one body: so also is Christ. (KJV)

2. The Fivefold Ministry Gifts: Ephesians 4: 11-16
And he gave some, apostles; and some, prophets; and some, evangelist; and some, pastors and teachers. For the perfecting of the saints, for the work of the ministry, for the edifying the body of Christ: Till we all come in the unity of the faith, and of the knowledge of the Son of God , unto a perfect man, unto the measure of the stature of the fullness of Christ: That we no more tossed to and fro as children carried about with every wind of doctrine , by the sleight of men, and cunning , craftiness, whereby they lie in wait to deceive ; But speaking the truth in love, may grow up into him in all things , which is the head, even Christ: from whom the whole body fitly joined together and compacted by that which every joint supply , according to the effectual working in the measure of the body unto the edifying of itself in love. (KJV)

3. The Office Gifts (Gifts of Administration):
Romans 12:4-8
For as we have many members in one body, and all member have not the same office; So we being many, are one body in Christ, and every one member one to another: Having then gifts differing according to the grace that is given that is given to us, whether prophecy let us prophesy according to the portion of faith. Or ministry, let us wait on our ministering: or he that teach on teaching; Or he that exhort, on exhortation: he that give, let him do it with simplicity; he that rule, with diligence; he that show mercy, with cheerfulness. (KJV)

God's Government for the Kingdom of God is not meat and drink; but righteousness, and peace, and joy in the Holy Ghost. – Romans 14:17

4. The Fruits of the Spirit:
The first fruit of the Spirit is Love. There should be an honest desire to love God with all our heart, mind and soul and love our neighbors as ourselves. Blessed are the pure in heart for they shall see God for the pure in heart and

perfect love cast out all fear. If we pursue the heart of God this fruit will develop in our life this is the first fruit in the Kingdom of God.

Joy-The Joy of the Lord is our strength and this joy I have the world didn't give it to me and the world can't take it away. We must have joy unspeakable joy even though we have our testing times, trials and temptations. His Joy will always be a comfort in time of need. The joy knowing that God is using you for His glory will keep us strengthen day by day the blessings of God.

Peace – This peace is like nothing you have experience before or will ever experience. This is an inner peace. This peace is a perfect peace. It is His peace, the Lord of peace, the prince of peace so all of the noise will cease and the confusion will stop. A peace that surpasses all understanding. It is a supernatural peace.

Peace I leave with you; my peace I give you. I do not give as the world gives. Do not let your heart be troubled and do not be afraid for Jesus is Lord and he cares for you. John 14:2

Patient This fruit may take time to develop, but the good news is that God is and will be patient with us. We will never fully arrive here on earth on this lifetime journey. Through love and patient has he drawn us. God is patient and He is the author of patience. The bible say patience is a virtue and some of us He has to work in us over time. But He will visit in dreams and His word is a sure way of getting patience. Be patient for God is not through with you yet.

Kindness-I practice an act of kindness everyday and sometimes I meet people that are less fortunate than me. I do an act of kindness to help at that time. The word state that we could be entertaining angels unaware. But just to do something for someone from your heart and expect nothing in return is one of the greatest joys in doing it. Love is kind so be kind!

Goodness- Goodness and mercy shall follow you all the days of my life.

Goodness is doing a good work in helping people so that they may glorify God for He is good all the time. The good works should point people to Jesus.

Faithfulness-When you are faithful to the call of God on your life whether in church or at home, God will honor our faithfulness.

Gentleness-The gentle soft voice of His spirit for He is a gentleman and He will always be in the spirit of meekness. Blessed are the meek for they shall inherit the earth. Even when we are right and sometimes wrong, He gives you the ability to be gentle.

Self- Control- We need self- control in all we do. Sometimes people reject some things the we say or do but God give us self- control to hold our tongue. Sometimes it is hard to control your tongue, your emotions, fears, insecurities. Self -Control is a fruit to exercise in the Kingdom of God.

Chapter 7
The Hands of God Ministry

All five are needed to perfected, matured and equip the saints "till we all come to the unity of the faith and the knowledge of the son of God, to a perfect man the fullness of Christ" (Ephesians 4: 11-12).

The Apostle: The Thumb
Apostle function in administration together with the prophets. They lay the foundation with proper doctrine and spiritual structure (Eph. 2:22). Apostle moves primarily in the gifts of healing, faith, working of miracles, word of wisdom, discerning of spirits and prophecy.

The Prophet: The forefinger
The forefinger is the pointer finger for the Prophets. Prophets function in revelation pointing the way for believers. The office of the Prophet carries a government authority role with a higher responsibility by giving instructions, rebuke, judgment, and revelation. Whatever Christ choose to speak through is for the purification and perfection of His church. Prophets are given a special ability to recognize God's gift and callings on individuals and activate people into their ministries.

The Evangelist: The middle finger
Evangelist represents the outreach ministry extended to evangelize the world. There is a vision for winning souls to Jesus and evangelists train prophetic evangelists.

Pastors- The ring finger
Pastor is committed to his flock. Prophets and Evangelist might come and go, but the pastor is bound to love and care for his flock. The Pastor is shepherding relationships. The Pastor performs weddings, funerals, visitations, prayers, counseling, and other ministerial duties.

The Teacher-The little finger
The Teacher grounds the Church in truth through instruction in the principles of the Word of God. The teaching department in a modern day church should oversee the educational and developing curriculum and performing teaching duties.

These are the governmental gifts in God's Kingdom to build up the Kingdom of God and bring this fallen world back into divine alignment before the fall of Adam and Eve. We must seek God's Kingdom violently! The government of God is with God, the Father, the Son and the Holy Spirit with each one doing work in and through us: The office gifts comes from the Father and the fivefold giftings comes from the Son, Jesus and the nine gifts of the Spirit comes from the Holy Spirit. This makes up the government of the kingdom of God and this is why the Word states that one must be born again in order to see the kingdom of God. You have to become a new creature with a new heart. This is why the body of Christ is out of order and we are not functioning like we are supposed to making us a dysfunctional boy. We are to make disciples. Jesus talked a lot about the Kingdom of Heaven and He said, "My kingdom was not of this world…." (John 18:36 KJV). We are to operate in this Kingdom under God's government. We are to walk by faith and not by sight (II Corinthians 5:7 KJV). Without faith it is impossible to please him; he who comes to him must believe that He is a rewarder those who diligently seek Him (Hebrews 11:6 KJV). Everything is done in the kingdom by faith and obedience unto to God —Jesus is our example and the Holy Spirit is our teacher.

Colors in Dreams

As we grow in our walk with God, because this is a faith walk. It is impossible to please God without faith. If we seek God for healing and He heals us our faith grows. We will be strengthening as we go from faith to faith. God gives each one of us a measure of faith. In your walk, everyone will not be able to go with you if their faith is not where your faith is in God. So what is faith you may ask? Faith is defined as belief with strong conviction, firm belief in something for which there maybe no tangible proof, complete trust, confidence, reliance or devotion. Faith is the opposite of doubt. Faith is the substance or assurance of things we hope for, but have not seen yet, or have not received. Faith comes before a prayer is answered or before an individual has received what he or she has requested.

Matthew 9:27-30 KJV Two blind men came to Jesus and asked Him to heal them and Jesus asked "Do you believe that I am able to do this?" They replied" Yes Lord." He touched their eyes saying, "According to your faith let it be unto you."

Three types of faith: The mustard seed faith, the gift of faith and the shield of faith.

A mustard seed is a very small seed and Jesus compared the kingdom of God to a mustard seed A seed carries within itself the DNA, the blueprint of the parent plant. An Apple tree produces an apple tree not a peach tree. A mustard seed is going to produce a mustard plant. The Word of God will produce the Kingdom of God within.

Luke 17:21 "Neither will they say, Lo here or lo there for, behold, the kingdom of God is within." Jesus talks about the kingdom of God as a living thing that grows within us to produce remarkable things. If you have faith the size of a mustard seed, you will say to this mountain, move from here to there, and it will move; and nothing will be impossible for you.

Jesus promises it will move, it shall come to pass and it will obey you. This is called Kingdom Authority. Jesus compares mustard to mountains and it only takes a mustard seed amount of faith in the Kingdom. Here is where we miss it. We have to speak to the mountain and say move here to there. We must open our mouth and speak those things out that we have inside our earthly vessel. The kingdom of God is within that mustard seed has to grow.

Unbelief- "Why we could not cast him out? And Jesus said unto them Because of your unbelief "(Matthew 17:20 KJV). The disciples wanted to cast out a demon, but they could not cast him out because of their unbelief. Only unbelief will stop us from doing the supernatural so we must deal with areas of unbelief by spending time with God. The disciples ask Jesus to increase their faith even though they had the word with them all the time. Jesus was doing all types of miracles, healings all manner of supernatural, but the disciple were not paying attention to what they really had in their mist. Jesus is the Living Word made manifest and dwell among us. Jesus was increasing their faith by all He did. For the Kingdom of God is not of meat or drink or anything natural but of love, joy and peace in the Holy Ghost.

Chapter 8
More Interpreting Your Dreams

We can get into myths where we think God is saying one thing, but He is speaking something totally different. Dreams and Interpretations are an ongoing learning experience in the Kingdom. I must express that Jesus did not come to teach and practice religion. What is religion? Religion is a mindset on something that we have learned and practice most of our life until we have a personal encounter with Jesus. I know this may be hard for some to take in, but it is true that we need to unlearn what we have learned from the world and our culture. I'm not saying that all is religion from our culture, but once we begin to follow the principles and practices of Jesus, our blinders come off.

1. **Dreams of Going to School**- If you see yourself taking a test it could mean a promotion, high school dream or dreams where you see yourself in a school or a class room setting. You are in school and the Holy Spirit is teaching you for that promotion in your life.

2. **Dreams of Various Vehicles**- These dreams may indicate the calling you have on your life. The vehicle of purpose that will carry you from one point to another. Example: cars, planes, buses any type of vehicle symbolize the type or even the size of your ministry. You are in ministry or you will engage in ministry. That's why in a dream there are different types of vehicles in your dream, because there are different types of ministry.

3. **Dreams of Storms**-Storms dreams tend to indicate intercessory spiritual warfare. These types are common for people who answer the call to intercessory prayer. The Gift of Discerning of Spirit.

4. **Dreams of flying**- Flying dreams deal with your spiritual capacity

to rise above problems and difficulties to soar into the heavenliness. These are some of the most inspirational and encouraging in tone of these dreams.

5. **Dreams of being naked or exposed**- These dreams you will be or you are becoming transparent or vulnerable depending on your particular situation. These dreams are meant to draw you into a greater intimacy with the Lord, and indicate places where greater transparency is required.

6. **Dreams of the condition of your teeth**- These dreams reveal the need for wisdom, teeth represent wisdom which could mean you need wisdom for something you are about to bite into. The fear of the Lord is the beginning of wisdom and knowledge of the Holy one which is the beginning of understanding. Proverbs 9:10

7. **Dreams of past relationship**- This type of dream may indicate that you are being tempted to fall back into old patterns and ways of thinking. Depends on who the person is in your past and what the person or people represent.

8. **Dreams of dying**- Dreaming about dying could mean something is passing away, dying in your life and in your flesh meaning God is putting it to death to bring something to life.

9. **Dreams of birth**- Dreaming about birth reveals a new season of purpose and destiny coming forth into your life and birthing something new.

10. **Dreams of Falling**-Common dreams is the fear of losing control. You are falling, but you never hit the ground meaning you need to get something in your life in control and that's why you need hit the ground in this dream.

11. **Dream of taking a shower**- These are cleansing dreams consist

of toilets, showers, and bathtubs. Revealing things that are in the process of being flushed out of your life, cleansed and flushed away. These are good dreams so enjoy the showers of God's love for you and His mercy. Get cleansed from the dirt of the world and its ways. Apply the blood of Jesus and get ready for a new day.

12. **Dreams of being chased**- Chasing dreams often reveal enemies that are at work coming against your life and purpose. We see a person coming and chasing you, but can't see who they are. These dreams could also mean God is chasing you. He will chase those who He loves to be part of the kingdom.

13. **Dreams of a relative dead, or alive**- These dreams indicate generational issues at work in your life. These are both blessing and cursed dreams. You will need to discern as the whether to accept the blessing or curse and deal with the generational issue. If your grandparents appear in the dream, find out and ask God What He is speaking to you concerning this thing. You could be the one He has call to break those generational curses.

14. **Dreams called nightmare**- Nightmare dreams are more frequent in children and new believers in Christ. These dreams could reveal generational enemies at work that need to be cut off. It is a call to stand against the enemy of fear.

15. **Dreams of Snakes**- Dreams of snakes reveal the serpent, the devil with his demonic hosts at work through accusation, lies and attacking your character. Spiders, bears, alligators, and frogs are the enemy at work in your life, family, home and, ministry.

16. **Dreams of Dogs and Cats**- Dogs in your dream usually indicates friendship since dogs are considered a man's best friend. They are loyal, protected friends but these dreams my reveal the dark side, such as growling, attacking, and biting. These sometimes reveal a friend who is about to betray you. Please do not get upset with your dog.

17. **Dreams of going through doors**-Dreams of going through doors means a change is coming. New ways, new opportunities, and new advancements. Dreaming of elevators and escalators indicate you are rising higher into your purpose.

18. **Dreams of clocks and watches**- These dreams reveal what time it is in your life, or the need for a wake-up call in the Body of Christ or in a nation. It is time to be alert and watchful being a watchman on the wall. Which watch are you on? In other words, it is time to pray or a call for prayer.

Chapter 9

Faith Connections To Dream Interpretations

Seek ye first The Kingdom of God and his righteousness and all these things shall be added unto you. Matthew 6:33(KJV)

Now that we have established this Kingdom business and not church business, we can move on from faith to faith in the Kingdom of God but this requires the supernatural. We will now look into the gift of faith.

The Gift of Faith: The special gift whereby the Spirit provides believers with extraordinary confidence in God's promises, power, and presence so that they can take heroic stands for the future of God's work in the church. The person with this gift is able to envision what God wants to happen and to be certain he is going to do it in response to prayer, even when there is no concrete evidence. Faith must be exercised with love. The gift of faith is a childlike faith in the believer to believe and trust in the promises of God. This faith can increase and grow as we trust in the Lord with all our heart and lean not to our own understanding.

Jude 1-20 "But you beloved, building up yourselves on your most holy faith, praying in the Holy Ghost" (KJV) Do you see how faith and praying go together? You can't have one without the other. This kind of faith grows also through the years of experiences of God's supernatural power and movement. This is the faithfulness of God. When we begin to see the supernatural move of God from the third realm; what you believe in begins to manifest in the natural. I believe this gift of faith grows and it is faith for healing, finance, miracles, your family, community and church. We begin to walk by faith and not by sight. This is another level in the Kingdom from faith to faith.

A Direct Connection to Faith

In the book of Matthew 15: 21-28, there was a woman from the area of Tyre, who came to Jesus concerning her daughter, who she said was grievously vexed by the devil. When the disciples came and said", Lord Do something she is troubling us." Jesus, said, "I am not sent but to the lost sheep of the house of Israel." And so, she then came directly to Jesus, "Lord helps me." And he said, "it is not right to take the children 's bread and to throw it to the dogs." True, Lord but the dogs, "she said, "eat the crumbs that fall from the master's table." And Jesus said unto her, O woman great is thy faith, be it unto you even as you will" And her daughter was made whole that very hour. This is a perfect example on how healing faith brought healing to her family.

This woman through faith contacted Jesus for herself. She didn't have time to call the elders of the church so she came in contact with faith through a circumstance in her home with her daughter. Get you a direct line to Jesus for yourself through faith.

More Symbols for interpretation of Dreams

Now we are going to look at the symbols for numbers. A. One –God as a unity, a source of new beginning.
- B. One Hundred- fullness, full measure, Children of Promise.
- C. One Thousand-Maturity
- D. Two-Sign for witness, testimony, or unity E. Twelve-Divine government, apostolic government.
- F. Ten- Law and order.
- G. Three- God the father, the son and God the Holy Spirit. H. Four- Worldwide, universal, four corners of the earth.
- I. Five- God's grace to man responsibility of man.
- J. Forty- testing, trial, closing in victory or defeat in the wilderness.
- K. Fourteen- Passover, time of testing.
- L. Six-number of man.

M. Seven- The year of completion.
N. Eight-New beginning.
O. Nine-Judgment, finality.
P. Ten-Law and Order.
Q. Eleven- Incomplete, disorder.
R. Twelve-Divine government.

These are just a few of the number symbols in our dreams and visions.

The Shield of Faith

The shield of faith is mention in the Armor of God of divine protection in Ephesians 6:16. On this faith, I had to do a quite a bit of research because this faith protects you from the evil attacks of the enemy. The shield is faith itself. Now because we are in a spiritual warfare, this shield protects the heart, the lower body from attacks that comes against your lower body and upper body especially your heart. Out of your heart comes the issues of life. This is so true for if the enemy knows what is in your heart, your dreams and visions, he will try to use them against you for bad.

Now faith is the substance of things hope for and the evidence of things not seen. Hebrew 11:1 KJV

The simple form of faith is believing God is faithful and truthful. If God says it in His Word, then we should believe what His Word says is true no matter what comes to distract us or if something does not come to pass when we want it to. Even though we are in a battle that has to be defeated in our lives, Jesus has already won the victory on the cross at Calvary. He will never leave us alone in the battle. He promises that He would never leave us nor forsake us. We must believe Him at us Word. We are not strong in our own weakness, defects, and flaws. This is why we have to give everything to God and let Him strengthen us when we fall short. Faith is the access to all we need to get from God, because without faith it is impossible to please him. Remember we don't need more faith just use the faith that you have then do something about it. Faith without works is dead meaning it's already done on earth as it is in heaven so walk in victory in the Kingdom of God. Our faith can and will be tested, but this faith will supernaturally quench the fiery darts of the evil one that attacks your body saying you are sick, you broke, and God wants you miserable. This faith will protect you in spite of what is going on in our lives. We don't need more faith but we need to know more truth. Jesus said, "The work we need to do was believe for the just shall live by faith". This is the kind of faith that shows up in the way we walk in the Kingdom. It is called Walking by Faith and not by what we see or by our circumstance.

What will you believe? Do you believe God gives grace and more grace? Use the faith to access the grace inside and act according to your faith.

Fiery Darts

The enemy shoot fiery darts everyday. You may ask, "What kind of fiery darts?" The enemy implants the following thoughts into your mind:

*Doubt – You ask yourself, 'Did I miss it or did God really say that or show me that?'
*Discouragement- The enemy says, "You're never going to be somebody. You will always be slow."
*Delay-You question your ability, "Why is this taking so long?"
*Depression-Don't feel like making effort in what you started.

All these are called fiery darts of the enemy. They come to us daily to create all these negative and uncertainty in your life. The shield of faith is the only protection you have against all these negative thoughts. We are to trust God in every step we take; when the storm come raging, take up that shield of faith. When trial and error comes take the shield of faith. When your children are out of control take up that shield of faith. It is all about faith in God, believing in just what He says in His Word about you. His thoughts are good toward you. This is what I love and discovered about God is that He wants the best for his people and is love, kind and longsuffering towards us.

Ephesians 6:10 Finally, you be strong in the Lord and in the strength of his might. 11. Put on the whole Armor of God that you may be able to stand against the schemes of the devil. 12. For we do not wrestle against flesh and blood, but against the rulers, against the authorities, against the cosmic power over this present darkness, against the spiritual forces in the heavenly places. 13. Therefore take up the whole Armor of God, that you may be able to withstand in the evil day, and having done all to stand firm. 14. Stand having put on the breastplate of righteousness, the belt of truth, the shoes for your feet, which is the gospel of peace, takes up the shield of faith.

Remember all of these go alone with prayer. There are three levels of faith that must have prayer to keep open communication and fellowship with God. Along with prayer, this will strengthen us as we see the supernatural manifest into the natural. I am told that there were seventy-two parables that Jesus spoke concerning the Kingdom of Heaven. The Kingdom must have been very important for Jesus to talk about. The attacks of the enemy come to kill, steal and destroy. He attacks the area that we are weak in and these fiery darts are not to be ignored; for they are real. This spiritual battle is real so we must stay connected to source to quench these fiery darts.

Visions

Visions are different from dreams. The difference is dreams happen while we are asleep and visions happen when you are awake. It is like being in a trance or looking at a picture movie, they are open visions while you are awake. Visions cause us to" see" beyond the natural realm. Visions may come in symbols or may be easy to understand and interpret but they are like watching a movie. One of Jesus disciples had a vision while he was awake and fell into a trance.

Acts 10-9:16 "The sky opened up, and a certain object like a great sheet coming down, lowered by four corners to the ground" (KJV). If visions come with symbols they should not be interpreted carelessly. Vision should be tested against scripture, because the demonic realm can also produce visions. Everything that God does the devil copies.

1 John 4:1" Beloved believe not every spirit, but test the spirits to see whether they are from God, because many false prophets have gone out into the world" (KJV). We need to test them, study them very thoroughly to see and understand what God is saying to you and me. We need not get into error with these gifts. We need not rush them but let us get teaching and training on the things of the Kingdom so we won't be accused of being false. God speaks through visions and the message will be visual. Maybe some of you have these open vision where you see pictures like on a movie screen and don't understand what is going on with you. Some call it being a seer.

Chapter 10

Revelations That John Saw in a Vision

Seeing in the spirit was not a rare thing for the Prophets of the Old Testament and New Testament. This is how the father communicated with them. He said, "See and then he said, "Write what you see", because open visions help you see into the spirit world. When John was in the Island Patmos, John was in the Spirit on the Lords' Day. If we can grasp the understanding of Dream and Visions and how God speaks with symbols, then our dreams and visions will become clear with clarity. Let's look at John who had open visions while he was in the Spirit and not in the flesh.

> ***Revelation 1:1 KJV The Revelation of Jesus Christ, which God gave unto him, to show unto his servants' things which must shortly come to pass; and he sent and signified it by his angel unto his servant John: 2. Who bare record of the Word of God, and of the testimony of Jesus Christ, and of all things that he saw. 3. Blessed is he that read and they that hear the words of this prophecy, and keep those things which there in: for the time is at hand.***

Listen to this Word and Prophecy. This is not about money, cars, houses, husbands and wives. The Word of this Prophecy is about revelations of things coming to pass in the Kingdom of God. John saw in the spirit in a vision that was reveal to him by God, not man. This is a one on one personal communication between God and his servant John. He gave instruction to write what you see so they that read it will understand and be blessed. The Prophecy and the Vision go together. Remember me saying earlier that interpretations are:

Prophecy, Word of Knowledge, Word of Wisdom and Visions.
God's Word promises that in the last days he will "pour out his Spirit upon all flesh: and your sons and daughters shall prophesy, you old men shall dream dreams, your young men shall see visions" (Acts 2:17). And also upon my servants and upon my handmaids in those days will I pour out my Spirit (Joel 2:29). This is why the enemy fight true children of the Kingdom of God so hard, because of the Kingdom Keys that Jesus gave to His people, which is what I have written about up unto now from hearing His voice to His Kingdom
Government. Jesus told Peter in Matthew 16: 18 that "upon the rock I will build my church and the gates of hell shall not prevail against it". The church of Jesus Christ is not a building made with hands but the Kingdom within with our body being the temple where God lives and dwells. We are to bring the Kingdom of Heaven to the earth realm to show the Love of God. It is time to operate in Kingdom Authority for the Kingdom of Heaven suffers violence and the violet takes it by force. – Matthew 12:11

Authority and Power are keys to the Kingdom of Heaven, but not to be strong and haughty in spirit. The keys of Authority and Power are to be cloth in humility. Where did we get the notion that exercising these keys over people is what Jesus was expressing? He said," I give you Authority to trample on snakes and scorpions and to overcome all the power of the enemy; and nothing will harm you." Wow snakes and scorpions! What was Jesus talking about? Well I would probably say we have people that have snake and scorpions features but with smiling faces. He said; "We will be able to overcome them with His help. I have learned that this power and authority comes with humbleness of heart because pride is an enemy of the soul and spirit.

Visions

"No man can look with undivided vision at God and at the world of reality so long as God and the world are torn asunder. Try as he may, he can only let his eyes wander distractedly from one to the other. But there is a place at which God and the cosmic reality are reconciled, a place at which God and man have become one. That and that alone is what enable man to set his eyes upon God and the world at the same time. This place does not lie somewhere out beyond reality in the realm of ideas. It lies in the midst of history as divine miracles. It lies in Jesus Christ, the reconciler of the world."

-----------DIETRICH BONHOEFFER

If Dreams and Visions are one way, the God Speaks to us then why do we need the Prophetic Ministry?

When someone has a dream or vision and someone claims to interpret that dream or vision then that person is bringing forth revelation where there is no revelation which is called fortunetelling. It is the shining of light in a dark place where the light comes on which is called revelation so the light of that revelation that comes forth in the Prophetic Ministry. This is why it is not good to let everyone who say they are Prophets to speak into your life. We are to try the Spirit by the Spirit. If the Interpretation do not line up with the scriptures with its symbols and parables, or witness with your Spirit then interpretation should not be accepted as a message from God speaking to the individual. We have to learn to test, study, and apply the true Word of God against these things so we will not be deceived by the cunning and crafting of men. I love truth. What about you?

Ephesians 1:17-18 (KJV) That the God of our Lord Jesus Christ, the Father of glory, may give unto you the spirit of wisdom and revelation in the knowledge of him: 18. The eyes of your understanding being enlighten; that ye may know what the hope of his calling is, and what the riches of the glory of his inheritance in the saints.

That the eyes of your understanding be enlighten (open). What eyes? Your spiritual eyes are called revelation as something that is being revealed to the understanding of your mind. To un-cover, bring forth truth and understanding. The revelation was given to John to write what he saw in his vision while he was awake. Visions happen while you are awake, but dreams happen when you are asleep. These are just a few examples of the difference between dreams and visions. I have given scripture example of real people in the bible that had real life experience to make a point clear that God spoke then, and He still speaks today, but we need to get the understanding of what He is saying to us through dreams and visions. All of these are part of The Mystery of the Kingdom of Heaven; for His Kingdom is a Mystery until He wants to reveal what He wants to reveal.

Daniel's Visions

In the first year of Bel-shaz'-zar, king of Babylon, Daniel had a dream and vision of his head up on his bed; then he wrote the dream, and told the sum of the matters. Daniel spoke and said,' I saw in my vision by night, and behold four winds of the heavens strove upon the great sea. And four great beasts came up from sea, diverse one from another. The first was like a lion, and had eagle's wings: I beheld till the wings thereof were plucked, and it was lifted up from the earth, and made stand upon the feet as a man, and a man's heart was given it. And behold another beast, a second, like to a bear, and it raised up itself on one side, and it had three ribs in the mouth of it between the teeth of it: and they said thus unto, Arise, devour much flesh' (Daniel1:1-5 KJV).

If we look into this vision of Daniel and the beasts that he saw in a vision is weird, but real enough that Daniel had to write it down. Journaling is a good way to remember your dreams and vision, because you can go back and read it over and over to try and make sense of the matter getting clarity of what the message that God is speaking to you about.

Then was the secret revealed unto Daniel in a night vision, and then Daniel blessed the God of Heaven. Daniel answered and said, 'Blessed be the name of God forever and ever: for wisdom and might are his: And he changed the times and the seasons: he removes kings, and set up kings: he gives wisdom unto the wise, and knowledge to them that no understanding: He reveal the deep and secret things: he knows what is in the darkness, and the light dwell with him. I thank thee, and praise thee, O you God of my fathers, who hast given me wisdom and might, and has made known unto me now what we desired of thee: for you have now made known unto us the king's matter. There Daniel went in unto Ar'-i-och, whom the king had ordained to destroy not the wise men of Babylon: bring me in before the king, and I will show unto the king the interpretation'. (Daniel 2:19-24)

This is for us today and another way that God speaks. God is speaking but are you listening? If we take time to study the scriptures, we will see that these people had trials, testing, trouble, complaints, sickness, illness mentally and physically, but God is a righteous God. No matter where you are in life, He will meet you there. Dreams and Visions with their interpretations are for us to develop, but not to make them the only way God speaks and worships them and get complete guidance from them. Just to know that a higher power that wants to communicate and fellowship with you should give you some peace of mind who He really is and want to be in your life, because He cares about every area of your life.

Write the Vision

Habakkuk 2: 1-4 – I Will stand upon my watch and set me upon the tower, and will watch to see what he will say unto me, and what I shall answer when I am reproved. 2. and the Lord answered me, and said, Write the vision, and make it plain upon tablets, that he may run that read it. 3. for the vision is yet for an appointed time, but at the end it shall speak, and not lie: though it tarry, wait for it; because it will surely come, it will not tarry. 4. Behold, his soul which is lifted up is not upright in him: but the just shall live by faith.

When You are called to write, you began to Journal and write down things you hear inside your spirit. You are just stepping out on faith not knowing where this will take you. Some keep diaries and some of us have a personal journal we write and write some more. People ask me; "What made you decide to write a book? I have always wanted to write a book because this have always been one of my passions. I was born to write which this is one of the purposes of God for people to do in the earth. I am family oriented so that means I spend the majority of my time alone. After so many trials in my family, the many rejections and hurts I experienced that I decided to spend my alone time writing. I just want to encourage some of you out there who may want to write a book that you don't have to be afraid to let go and let God. Don't be afraid to step out on faith for it will take a brave heart that will please God when it is all said and done. We are to be doers of the word and not just hearers only. We are to apply the Word to our life and our circumstances.

Chapter 11

Giftings

I believe that we were all created and born to dream. We are unique people with different gifts and talents born to win and be champions to conquer and change the world. I believe that no two people are the same. Sometimes when we meet someone who is different, we tend to think they are strange or weird. God does not make mistakes, because we are looking at the outside and not looking within. Some are rejected, put down, thrown down, but God created man in His image. The main people we ignore, and push to the side are the ones who God has gifted. Most people that we see alone are the ones who are able to hear the voice of God. Think about it. Who do they talk to the most? It seems like they are talking to themselves, but in reality they are talking to either a good spirit or a bad spirit. What I am saying is dreams enrich our life by giving us encouragement, direction, insight and revelation. I get much of my personal revelation through words meaning that I write what I hear. I write it down on paper but I also dream and have many visions. Everyone needs a vision and we need to be people of purpose and destiny. Those who dream aim high and soar above all limitations.

Proverbs 29:18- *Where there is no vision the people perish: but he that keep the law, happy is he (KJV).*

You were created in God's very image to have a supernatural spiritual gift that is on the inside of you that needs to be trained and developed but all you have to do is tap into it. Learn who you are and what your purpose for being born is. God speaks through dreams and vision, but as I have pointed out early in this book we are not to idolize the gift, but to worship the gift giver in order to flourish. This is where mankind got off on the wrong track because we are too busy giving more attention to the gift than the one who gives the gift that we become Idol worshippers. These studies of information are not meant to give you the ideal to idolize your dreams and vision, nor give more attention to them than you do your creator but meant for you to point you towards God. When I first came into the knowledge that my dreams and visions were from God meaning and that He was speaking to me through them that I got very excited but I had to realize that I was not to make them my god. This was not hard for me because I love to read so reading the Word alone with my dreams made this journey easy and exciting. When we learn about the mysteries and the unknown, it gets real exciting, because we are exploring new territory. The gift opens way for the giver but there is always a cost and if we want to move into areas of the supernatural or move in the gift(s) that are inside of us then there is a price to pay. There is a cost and a battle we must fight in order to win. What does it cost? You have to lose your reputation, you have to lose your traditions, and you have to lose your religion. Religion and tradition is a mindset. In order to move in God with the gift, we have to move in Him and in His revelation.

Proverb18:16- A man's gift makes room for him, and brings him before great men (KJV).

Let us stir up the gifts that God has place inside of us because the Kingdom of Heaven is within us and God is speaking today through dreams and visions. The kingdom will be advance through them. I really admire gifted talented people. I love being around them. I appreciate their energy, the confidence, their spunk, and determination. These are the people that will help you get from one level to the next.

Encouragers:

Everyone loves to get a word of praise or encouragement. To some of us it helps us to know that what we are doing is being appreciated. Some have the gift to see into your life and that there is something on the inside of you that needs to be birth out. It is a gift that these people have to see into your life. Have you ever been around someone who could see into your life what you could not see? I have come into contact with many people in my life, but I didn't understand any of it at the time. We have a tendency to take advantage of these special people just because we think they are nuts. But in reality they are place in your life by God for either short term or long term to help us get to our next level but sometimes we rebel against the person who God sent to help us. They are the encouragers that come to help you stay on the right road, but we rebel and walk away never to see them again for a long period of time or maybe never again. We are all called and born for ministry either to minister and to be ministered to. As I said early, please don't let the word minister get you disturbed. We all have a ministry if we have children, husband, a teacher, own a business and etc. Ministry is not just behind a pulpit ministry but starts a home training a child in the way he should go and when he is old he will not depart from it. Ministry is teaching; caring, sharing, encouraging, and helping to build up ministry is love. Some of us need tough love too so there is those who are sent to us to minister to us tough love.

Write Down Your Dreams

How important are dreams to God? According to The late John Paul Jackson one-third of the bible is devoted to dreams, vision, and prophecy. Writing down your dreams creates a record you can look back on and go over what you have dreamed in detail. The words you use in writing, your dream will help with the interpretation. It helps you to value and build your faith in what you learn and how you learn. Dreams are an open door for God to get you attention and to invite you into a relationship with Him, because the more you dream and want to understand, the more you will search for information to understand. Since He created you and knows all of your strength and weakness only He knows how to get our attention. As I stated early, we are not to just pursue dreams as guidance only. We are to pursue the giver of the gift primarily through His Word. The process of understanding dreams and interpreting dreams is head knowledge of what you learn and spirit knowledge of what the spirit of God is telling you about the dream. There will be symbolism, pictures, colors, and numbers in order to learn to interpret but you will have to study the symbols, pictures, colors, and numbers to understand most of your dreams.

> *Man does not live on bread alone but by every word that comes from the mouth of God. Deuteronomy 8:31*
>
> *Give ear and come to me; listen, that you may live. Isaiah 55:3*

We are not less than the men or women of God in the Bible! We can develop an intimate heart-to-heart relationship with God as well, if we truly want to.

The Mystery of it All

The Mystery of the Kingdom is give unto you these mysteries of the Kingdom which are all in Christ. The Mystery that has been kept hidden for ages and generation. For those who recognize Christ can discover all the treasures of wisdom and knowledge and know the secrets of the kingdom of heaven. We are in a blessed state to be able to know the Secrets of the Kingdom and to understand that Christ is the Mystery of the Kingdom. This is why we are not to lose focus on the gift giver and idolize the gift without the Word. Jesus is the Word that lives on the inside of us who brings our spirit alive because He is the living Word, active, and alive. The Word and the gift go hand and hand and He is the Mystery of the Kingdom. We have to discover all the treasures of His wisdom and knowledge knowing that the mystery is given unto us for those who believe in Him. Jesus came to earth in an ordinary way; He came in the likeness of a human just like one of us, and His life was no different than the lives of ordinary people. He came down to experience the same things that we go through in life. He suffered, he was rejected, he was talked about and he was beaten, so the people did not recognize him.

John 6:41-45
At this the Jews began to grumble about him, because he said, I am the bread that came down from heaven. "The said, "Is this not the Jesus, the son of Joseph and Mary whose father and mother we know? "How

can he now say, I came down from heaven?" Jesus answered, "No one can come to me unless the father who sent me draws him, and I will raise him up at the last day. It is written in the Prophets they will all be taught by God; everyone who listens to the father and learns from him comes to me."

To those who did not believe Jesus was only seen as the son of Joseph and Mary. They rejected him seeing as a natural man from a common family but no so in the supernatural.

In A Night Vision

The secret was revealed unto Daniel in a night vision. Then Daniel answered and said, "Blessed be the name of God forever and ever. For wisdom and might are his: And he changes the times and the season: he removes kings, and set up kings: he gives wisdom unto the wise, and knowledge to them that no understanding: He reveal the deep and secret things: he knows what is in the darkness, and the light dwell with him. I thank you and praise you, the God of my fathers, who have given me wisdom and might, and has made known unto me now what we desired of you: for thou has now made known unto us the king's matter".
(Daniel 2:19-23 KJV)

The Interpretation of the Dream

Daniel answered in the presence of the king, and said, "The secret which the king has demanded cannot the wise men, the astrologers, the magicians, the soothsayers, show unto the king Nebuchadnezzar what shall be in the latter days. The dream, and the visions of your head upon your bed, are these; As for you O king your thoughts came unto your mind upon your bed, what should come to pass hereafter: and he that reveal secrets make known to you what shall come to pass. But as for me, the secret is not revealed to me for any wisdom that I have more than any living, but for their sakes that shall make known the *interpretation to the king, and that you mightiest know the thoughts of your heart. Thou, O king, saw, and behold a great image, whose brightness was excellent, stood before you; and the form thereof was terrible. This image's head was of fine gold, his breast and his arms of silver, his belly and his thighs of brass, His legs of iron, his feet part of iron and part clay. You saw till that a stone was cut out without hands, which smote the image upon his feet that were of iron and clay, and break them to pieces. Then was the iron, the clay, the brass, the silver, and the gold, broken to pieces together, and became like the chaff of the summer threshing-floors; and the wind carried them away, that no place was found for them: and the stone that smote the image became a great mountain, and filled the whole earth. This is the dream; and we will tell the interpretation thereof before the king" (Daniel 2:27-36 KJV).*

The Prophet Daniel explained how the dreams and the interpretations because of a visitation from God through night visions or parables and dreams. God has always spoken to us in dreams, but we did not understand the meaning of them until the last days before Christ returns. In this day and time, He is giving us directions, guidance, warning and even laughter in dreams for God has a sense of humor as well. God cares for His children enough to speak to us even in dreams. Maybe you dream, but you don't remember your dreams but we all have dreams. If you don't remember them, you are missing out on one of the most beautiful ways God speak because you are missing out on experiencing His presence in a different way and waking up being refreshed through dreams. If you don't dream or remember your dreams is not to put you to shame, but there is another way which God speaks to you and it is not through dreams. We will not be approached by God in the same way, but we are all unique in His eyes. After God revealed the "Mystery "of the interpretation of the king's dream to Daniel, he gave thanks and praises to God who knows the intent of the human heart. I love the healing dreams, because God heals even the deep, deep hurts of the past. Daniel gave his praise and did not take the glory for giving the interpretation of the king's dream. He was humble in all he did in Babylon.

Am I a God at hand, said the Lord, and not a God afar off? Can any hide him in secret places that I shall not see him? Said the Lord Do not I fill heaven and earth? Said the Lord I have heard what the prophets said, that prophesy lies in my name, saying, I have dreamed, I have dreamed. How long shall this be in the heart of the prophets that prophesy lies? Yea, they are prophets of deceit of their own heart; Which think to cause my people to forget my name by their dreams which they tell every man to his neighbor, as their fathers have forgotten my name for Ba'-al. The prophet that has a dream, let him tell a dream; and he that has my word, let him speak my word, let him speak my word faithfully. What is the chaff to the wheat? Is not my word like as a fire? Said the Lord; and like a hammer that breaks the rock in pieces? (Jeremiah 23:23-29 KJV).

God is doing a new thing in the earth but it is not new to Him, but it is new to us because He is fed up with all of these false fake phony people that call themselves prophets. This may sound a little harsh, but it is true because it is either a money or entertainment gospel that they are preaching not the gospel of Jesus Christ. God desire for all His children to dream and learn to interpret their dreams, so He will speak to you concerning your purpose, destiny and the way you should take, but He will confirm in your spirit through others what He has spoken to you. Play church is over and it is time to get real with the creator of the universe. If you are running from church to church, conference to conference waiting for someone to speak to you concerning you; I would say you are wasting your time. Only the Creator have the answers to your purpose and destiny. If you observe the messages in your dreams He gives to you, seek them out and you will be totally satisfied if God speaks to you in dreams and visions. The reason I am so passionate about this Word is because God is ready to reveal Himself to all who diligently seek Him. He wants to talk with you and to Him be the glory.

Chapter 12

God's Kingdom

The Kingdom Citizen of the Kingdom

KINGDOM- a country, state, or territory ruled by a king or queen.

The word has the prefix 'King' which is one who rules over a country, state, or territory. Every kingdom must have a king and every king is automatically a lord over the kingdom. The reason we in the western country are not familiar with kingdoms because kingdoms have been part of other cultures in the world except for the United States. Kings and kingdoms were set up and kings ruled, but now because of Jesus Christ we are made kings and priests of a royal priesthood, because the kingdom is now within, and Jesus governs the kingdom. Here in the United States we have presidents not kings, but we are citizens of the kingdom where Jesus is Lord in this kingdom. I have only found this word 'Lord' in the bible. The President is voted in, but the king is positioned by birthright. It is said that all kings are automatically lords. Now look at the word 'Dom' comes from the word domain which represents a territory, or the geographical area in the western society. We have not had the privilege to live among kings and kingdoms. From my studies of kingdom, we can look into the Southern Kingdom and Northern Kingdom which were ruled by kings and most of them failed God. We will look into these two Kingdoms in depth in another chapter but for now we will focus on Kingdom citizenship. It is important that we understand the Mystery of the Kingdom for there is power in the Word for those who have been seeking the things of the kingdom.

Now Abraham and Sarah were old and well stricken in age; and it ceased to be with Sarah after the manner of woman. Therefore, Sarah laughed with in herself saying, after I am waxed old shall I have pleasure, my lord being old also? (Genesis 18:11-12 KJV).

God told Abraham that he and Sarah would have a child in their old age. When Abraham told Sarah she laughed, but when she asked the question should she have pleasure my lord, she was talking to Abraham for she called him Lord. This history of the Jewish people begins with Abraham in the Middle East where kings and kingdoms were set up. God told Abraham to leave his country and be obedient unto him that he would make him a father of many nations. Looking into history Abraham was called Abram was born in the 1813 month of Jewish calendar, Nissan. His father's name was Torah who was seventy years old when Abraham was born. Abraham's mother 's name was Amathlaah. The town in which he was born was called Cutha, in Mesopotamia. In the Torah, Abraham 's birth place is called Everhanahar ("Beyond the River"). Abraham was the tenth generation removed from Noah, being a direct descendant of Shem, (Noah's son), the father of all the "Semitic" people. When Abraham was born, Shem was 390 years old, and Shem's father Noah was 892 years old. Abraham was 58 years old when Noah died. These are important facts, for, as we shall see later, Abraham spent many years in the house of Noah and Shem and received instruction from them. Abraham learned all the details about the flood from the men who built the Ark. Torah, Abraham's father, was the chief officer or minister of the first mighty King Nimrod of Babylon also known as Shinear, and the land of the Chaldees. Torah was an idol worshipper, like his king, and their chief god was Sun. This is some of Abraham 's history in the middle east. Abraham was faithful and obedient to God who did not follow after idols as his father did. I think he was a king because we know that his wife Sarah called him Lord.

The Interpretation of the Dream

1 Samuel 25:23 KJV
And when Abigail saw David, she hasted, a lighted off the donkey, and fell before David on her face, and bowed herself to the ground. And fell at his feet, and said, upon me, my lord, upon me let this iniquity be: and let your handmaid, I pray speak in your audience, and hear your handmaid. Let not my Lord, I pray to you regard this man of

Belial, even Nabal: for as his name is, so is he; Nabal is his name, and folly is with him: but I your handmaid is with him: but your handmaid saw not the young men of my Lord, whom you did send. Now therefore the Lord live, and as your soul live, see the Lord has withheld you from coming to shed bleed, and from avenging yourself with your own hand, now let your enemies, and they that seek evil to my Lord, be as Nabel. Abigail called him Lord for David was a king so Lordship came automatic with the territory since this was the custom for Kingdom citizenship.

When Jesus talked about the Kingdom, they understood Kingdom principles and He would teach these principles through parables. Parables stories with spiritual lessons-these stories often deal with the kingdom.

The Interpretation of the Dream

Matthew 13: 18-23 KJV
Hear you therefore the parable of the sower. When any hear the word of the Kingdom, and understand it not, then come the wicked one, and catch away that which was sown in his heart, this which received seed by the way side. But he that received the seed into stony places, the same is he that hear the word, and anon with joy received it; Yet hath he not roots in himself, but endure for a while: for when tribulation or persecution arise because of the word, by and by he is offended. He also that receives seed among the thorns is he that hears the word; and the care of this world, and the deceitfulness of riches, choke, the word, and he became unfruitful. But he that receive seed into the good ground is he that hear the word, and understand it; which bear fruit, and bring forth, some a hundred fold, some sixty, some thirty.
Another parable he spoke to them saying, "The kingdom of heaven is like unto a man which sowed good seed in his field: But while men slept, his enemy came and sowed tares among the wheat, and went his way. But when the blade was sprung up, and brought forth fruit, then appeared the tares also. So the servants of the household made and said unto him, sir did not you sow good seed in your field? From where

then has it tears? He said unto them, an enemy has done this. The servants said unto him, will you then that we go and gather them up? But he said, no; let while you gather up the tears, you root up also the wheat with them. Let both grow together until the harvest: and in the time of harvest I will say to the reapers, gather you together first the tears, and bind them in bundles to burn them: but gather the wheat into my barn" (Matthew 13: 24-30 KJV).

He spoke in parables spiritual lessons for practical application for our life concerning the Kingdom. The Kingdom of Heaven is a Mystery but we can know the Mystery if we seek the Mystery of the Kingdom.

Seek Ye First the Kingdom of God and His Righteousness

Jesus came to Galilee, preaching the gospel of the Kingdom of God. The gospel is the good news so Jesus came preaching good news about the Kingdom of Heaven. As we seen earlier in the interpretation that Daniel had given to the King that this was an explanation of how the Kingdom of God would be established in the earth. Daniel interpreted the dream for the king and the dream was a prophecy to be fulfilled in the future which are called an internal prophetic dreams. God gave Daniel and his three friends, knowledge, skill and understanding. Daniel had understanding in all visions and dreams (Daniel 1:17). They found him to be ten times better than all the magicians and astrologers. Daniel prophesied as he was moved by the spirit of God through dreams and visions about what was going to happen throughout history.

- Four world-ruling empires- In a dream that Nebuchadnezzar dreamed, God revealed through Daniel that there would be four world-ruling empires (Daniel2:1-4:3). These are the Babylonian, Medo-Persian, Greco- Macedonian and Roman Empires. These empires were represented by four beasts.

- The Kingdom of God- After telling the King that there would be four world-ruling Kingdoms. Daniel prophesied: "And in the days of these kings during the time of human government the God of heaven will set up kingdom which shall never be destroyed; and the kingdom shall not be left to other people; it shall not be left to other people; it shall break in pieces and consume all these kingdoms, and it shall stand forever" – Daniel 2:44

- Little horn- In God's vision to Daniel of four beasts, representing four world ruling kingdoms, the fourth beast "had ten horns" Daniel 7:7 – this represent the fourth kingdom.

All of these are Mystery of the Kingdom of God which are the dreams, vision, prophecy, wisdom, knowledge and understanding of the Kingdoms in the Old and New Testament. These where written by men of God as the Spirit of God move upon them. When I begin to study about The Mystery of the Kingdom, the more curious I became with Kingdoms and how they operate or operated. The deeper I dig the more I wanted to know. I wanted to understand Kingdoms and if the subject was important to Jesus than surely He wanted us to understand how the Kingdom works and what the kingdom is all about which became a conviction for me.

Daniel 1:17 KJV
As for these four children, God gave them knowledge and skill in all learning and wisdom: and Daniel had understanding in all visions and dreams.

Chapter 13

God's Kingdom Covenant

The Land Flowing with Milk and Honey

God promises to bless those who obey Him. The Mosaic Covenant was named after Moses which was a covenant between God and the Israelites. This was a conditional covenant made between God and the nation of Israel at Mount Sinai (Exodus 19-1-6). On the third new moon after the people had gone out of the land of Egypt on that day, they came into wilderness of Sinai. They set out from Rephidim and came into the wilderness of Sinai, and they encamped in the wilderness. There Israel encamped before the mountain, saying, "Thus you shall say to the house of Jacob, and tell the people of Israel. You yourselves have seen what I did to the Egyptians, and how I bore you on eagles' wings and brought you to myself. Now therefore if, you will indeed obey my voice and keep my covenant, you shall be my treasured possession among all peoples, for all the earth is mine and you shall be to me a kingdom of priest and a holy nation. In the wilderness, God spoke to His people after He brought them out of bondage from the land of Egypt and immediately made a covenant with them. In return, He promises them they would possess the land flowing with milk and honey. The covenant serves as a nation set apart from other nations. This was a blood covenant was conditional blessing and cursing.

Deuteronomy 28: 1-14 KJV
And it shall come to pass, if you shall hearken diligently unto the voice of the Lord your God, to observe and to do all his commandments which I command you this day, that the Lord your God will set thee on high above all nation.

Blessed shall you be in the city, and blessed shall you be in the field. Blessed shall be the fruit of your body, and the fruit of your ground, and the fruit of your cattle, the increase of the kind, and the flocks of thy sheep.

Blessed shall be your basket and your store

Blessed shall you be when you come in, and blessed shall you be when you go out.

The Lord shall cause your enemies that rise up against you to be smitten before your face: they shall come out against you one way, and flee before you seven ways.

The Lord shall command the blessing upon you in your store houses, and in all that you set your hand to do; and he shall bless you in the land which the Lord your God give you.

The Lord shall establish you a holy people unto himself, as he has sworn unto you, if you shall keep the commandments of the Lord your god, and walk in his ways.

And all people of the earth shall see that you are called by the name of the Lord; and they shall be afraid of you.

And the Lord shall make the plenteous in goods, in the fruit of your body, and in the fruit of your ground, in the land which the Lord swore unto your fathers to give thee.

The Lord shall open unto you good treasure, the heaven to give rain unto your land in his season, and to bless all the work of your hand: and you shall lend unto many nations, and you shall not borrow.
And the Lord shall make you the head and not the tail; and shall be above only, and you shall not be beneath; if that you hearken unto the commandments of the Lord your God, which I command you this day, to observe and to do them:

And you shall not go aside from any of the words which I command you this day, to the right, or to the left, to go after other gods to serve them.

Disobedient Brings on the Cursing

Deuteronomy 28:15-25 KJV
But it shall come to pass, if you will not listen unto the voice of the Lord You God, to observe to do all his commandments and his statutes which I command you this day; that all these curses shall come upon you, and over take you:

Cursed shall you be in the city, and cursed shall you be in the field. Cursed shall be your basket and your store.

Cursed shall be the fruit of your body and the fruit lf your land, the increase of you kine, and the flocks of your sheep.

Cursed shall you be when you come in, and cursed shall you be going out.

The Lord shall send upon you vexation, and rebuke, in all that thou set your hand unto for to do, until you be destroyed, and until you perish quickly; because of the wickedness of your doings, whereby you have forsaken me.

The Lord shall make pestilence cleave unto you, until he has consumed you from off the land, where you go to possess it.

The Lord shall smite you with consumption, and with a fever, and with an inflammation, and with an extreme burning, and with the sword, and with blasting, and with mildew, and they shall pursue you until you perish.

And the heaven that is over your head shall be brass, and the earth that is under you shall be iron.

The Lord shall cause you to be smitten before your enemies: you shall go out one way against them, and flee seven ways before them:
and shall be removed into all the kingdoms of the earth.

I will stop here and you can read the rest of the cursing of disobedience in the chapter of Deuteronomy. There are those who oppose these curses for today but if you look around, ask yourself how much of the blessing do you see than the curses? I want the blessing of milk and honey that was promised by the Lord. Remember we said a Lord is over His territory. If Lords and Kings in the kingdom can give decrees and promises, how much more can the Lord of the heavens and the earth give us in our promise land? Even though these are written in the bible among the patriarch of old, we can have much more in the new through Christ Jesus, a new and better covenant with better promises through His blood. All we have to do is believe and have faith in the God of the Bible not in other gods who we know not of, but the Holy one of Israel. This is where we are falling short believing and listen diligently to His voice. He speaks in many ways to us. He is not far off from you but He is a God at hand if only you will believe He wants to have a personal relationship with you. I come to you with dreams and visions, because this is becoming a common thing among the people of God. Again I say these go alone with His Word and not to be worshiped as gods. What I am trying to get us to see is that Kingdom is also a mindset as is religion. God is calling us to change our thinking about who we are in Christ. I know some of us go to church three to four times a week, but we are not going anywhere if we are like the children of Israel going around and around and around in the wilderness with the same old mind set as a child. He is trying to retrain and reeducate us of the things of the kingdom. He speaks clearly through dreams and visions. Now we have gotten down how God speaks through His Word by the Holy Spirit, but He will speak to you individually in your dreams while you are asleep. God is tired of all the false Prophets who come in sheep clothes, but inwardly they are ravenous wolves. You can know without a shatter of doubt when a false Prophet is in your mist, but the same thing the Prophet operate in you can operate in too. I know some will be upset with me for telling the truth, but the truth will set us all free. If any come to you with the Word of God then they are coming with truth, because His Word is truth.

Chapter 14
More Dream Symbols, Faith, and Mysteries of the Kingdom

Symbolic Languages

The book of Revelation contains symbolic language, giving a description of the Messiah, the Son of Man, standing in the mist of seven Lamp stands, he had in his right hand seven stars, out of his mouth went a sharp two-edged sword, and His countenance was like the sun shining in its strength. (Revelation 1:16)

The Mystery of the Seven Stars:
What do they mean?

a. Stars are angels of the seven churches
b. Seven lamp stands are the seven churches
c. Statues are symbols of empire

What I am saying is dreams, visions and the Word of God all go together but it is hard to have one without the other. This is why it is good to read you bible for yourself because deception is on the rise. In dreams and visions, symbols, pictures, colors, and numbers are keys to interpret dreams, visions, and the word. Ever since I have these dreams and vision and compare them by studying the Word of God, I have gotten clarity, guidance and direction in my life in areas where I was confused the most. Believe me when I say there is a purpose for everything under the sun and that purpose is to safely get you to your destiny that you were born and created to do. I can see clearly now that the rain is gone. Don't you want to know what God is speaking to you about you? Don't you want to know the direction He has for you? Then follow your God given dreams and listen to the one who created you to dream.

Jeremiah 29:11-13 KJV For I know the thoughts that I think toward you, said the Lord, thoughts of peace, ad not of evil, to give you an expected end. Then shall you call me and you shall go and pray unto me and I will listen to you. And you shall seek me; and find me, when you shall search for me with all your heart.

Write the words in a book

The word that came to Jeremiah from the Lord, saying, Thus speaks the Lord God of Israel, saying, Write thee all the words that I have spoken unto you in a book. For , lo the days come, said the Lord,, that I will bring again captivity of my people Israel and Judah, said the Lord and I will cause them to return to the land that I gave to their fathers, and they shall possess it. And these are the words that the Lord spoke concerning Israel and concerning Judah. Jeremiah 30:1-4 KJV

I can't stress this too much for the kingdom is within, that's why we call Jesus Lord. The kingdom is within us for we were made in the image of God for He is the creator of all things and of all. He gave us dominion over everything in the earth, not over a human being, but dominion over land, the flower, of the air, fish in the sea and over everything else except people.

We need to learn to understand kingdom and kingdom principle. Maybe this unfamiliar to you and it was unfamiliar to me to when I first heard teaching on this, but the more I read about Jesus talking about the Kingdom that I begin to become familiar with Kingdom in the Bible. There were kings who started out good and ended up bad. These kings were over kingdoms in the middle east during biblical times. They reigned as they pleased. King Solomon, David's son, was one who started out great when he asked God for wisdom so he could rule over the people of Israel as a wise king.

1st King 3:3 KJV and Solomon loved the Lord, walking in the statues of David his father: only sacrificed and burnt incense in high places. And the king went to Gibeon to sacrifice there; for that was the great high place: a thousand burnt offerings did Solomon offer upon that altar. In Gibeon the Lord appeared to Solomon in a dream by night: and God said, ask what I shall give thee. And Solomon said, you have showed unto your servant David my father great mercy, according as he walked before you in truth, and in righteousness, and in uprightness, and in uprightness of heart with you; and you have kept for him this great kindness, that you have given him a son to sit on his throne, as it is this day.

I can go on and on with scriptures where dreams and visions were common among kings and prophet but it has been my conviction to help people of today through dreams, visions, the word and interpretation. I am convinced that God wants you to know Him in this way but He also don't want you to go to another source to tell you who you are and the purpose for you being born. Only He knows who you are and what you are made of. He is the only one who can tell you who? What? And Why? Trust me on this one I grew up in what they call holy roller, my Big mama, who name was Camilla Jones, who was a God fearing woman now before I came alone as her granddaughter. I have no idea what type of life she lived but all I know as a child is that we went to church on Sundays all day long until night fall. I was the first grandchild to be born so I receive a lot of attention from my mother side and dad side with all my uncles and auntie showering me with love. While this life style was not new to me when I grew up in it, I knew she was also a praying woman.

Proverbs 22:6 KJV
Train up a child in the way he should go and when he is old, he will not depart from it.

Faith, Hope and Love

I would not do you justice if I share with you all of the gifts, and not share with you in order for us to operate in the things of the Kingdom.

We need the most three important ingredients which is love, faith and hope. I will share them with you one at a time we need these to truly operate effectively in the kingdom.

But now abide faith; hope and love, these three, and the greatest is love. (1 Corinthians 13:13 KJV).

We know without faith it is impossible to please God and He that comes to Him must believe that He rewards those who diligently seek him meaning you are always looking, seeking, watching, waiting for Him. Faith is the substance of things hope for and the evidence of things not seen. For the just shall live by faith and not by what we see. What we see in temporary and it is the things we can't see that we should believe in. Do you ever wonder why God chose for us to walk, talk, and live by faith? Now I am not going to say I have faith like this at all times. Sometimes it can be difficult to walk by faith, because we are afraid of the unknown and what we can't see, or touch but faith is the key to unlocking the doors to all that God has for us. Abraham was a man of faith and the bible says it was counted unto him as righteousness.

HEBREW 11: 2-9 For by it the elders obtained a good report.

3. through faith we understand that the worlds were framed by the word of God, so that the things which are seen were not made of things which do appear.

4. by faith Abel offered unto God a more excellent sacrifice than Cain, by which he obtained witness that he was righteous, God testifying of his gifts: and by it he is yet speak.

5. by faith Enoch was translated that he should not see death; and was not found, because God had translated him: for before his translation he had this testimony, that he pleased God.

6. but without faith it is impossible to please him; for he that come to God must believe that he is, and that he rewards those that diligently seek him.

7. By faith Noah, being warned of God of things not seen as yet, moved with fear, prepared an ark to the saving of his house; by the which he condemned the world, and became heir of the righteousness which is by faith.

9. By faith he sojourned in the land of promise, as in a strange country, dwelling in tabernacles with Isaac and Jacob, the heirs with him of the same promise.

We see the heroes of faith through faith as they obtained a good report, so it is impossible to please Him without faith.

Hope

Hope makes you not ashamed, but that hope must be anchored in something or someone. Hope is an inspiring Word.
Hope is like reservoir of emotional belief in God.

- If I am put down I look for emotional reservoir of hope for the strength to return good for evil. Without hope, I have no power to know wrong and walk in love.

- If I experience setbacks in my plan or if I get sick, or things don't go my way; I find hope and look for strength to keep going and not give up.

- If I face temptation of any kind to steal, to lie or just plain lust for something, I look to my emotional reservoir of hope for the strength to hold fast to the way of righteousness, and deny myself some brief unsatisfying pleasure.

We should focus our attention and our hope in Him for He will fill our desire with overflowing. That deep down in the depths of our soul, there is this hope that we can depend on. A hope that will not make you ashamed.

Love

1 Corinthians 13:1-9 KJV

> *1. THOUGH I speak with the tongues of men and of angels, and have not charity, I am become as a sounding brass, or a tinkling cymbal.*
>
> *2. And though I have the gift of prophecy, and understand all mysteries, and all knowledge; and though I have all faith, so that I could remove mountains, and have not charity, I am nothing.*
>
> *3. And though I bestow all my goods to feed the poor, and goods to feed the poor, and though I give my body to be burned, and have not love, it profits me nothing.*
>
> *4. Charity(love) suffer long, and is kind; charity do not envy; charity do not vaunt itself, is not puffed up,*
>
> *5. Doth not behave itself unseemly, seek not her own, is not easily provoked, think no evil.*
>
> *6. Do not rejoice in inequity, but rejoice in truth;*
>
> *7. Bear all things, believe all things, hope all things, and endure all things.*
>
> *8. Charity never fails: but whether there are prophecies, they shall fail; whether there are tongues, they shall cease; whether there is knowledge, it shall vanish away.*
>
> *9. For we know in part, and we prophesy in part.*

For this is Love from the bible perspective and I couldn't leave out these three because if we have all these gifts and talents in operation and not have faith, hope, and love in our life; it profits us nothing. God is love, He is faithful, He is graceful, and to be an imitator of Him; we have to have Love.

More Dream Symbols

ARMOR: Spiritual Warfare.

AUTOMOBILE: Life or Ministry

BABY: New beginning, new idea.

BAT: Fear, or Witchcraft.

BED: Intimacy, peace, marriage.

BICYCLE: Works of the flesh.

BLOOD: Blood of Jesus, anger or stop.

BREAD: Bread of life.

CANDLE: Light, Holy Spirit.

CAT: Unclean, deception.

CORN: Symbolize oil, wine.

DOG: Hypocrites.

DRUGS: Spell, witchcraft.

ELEVATOR: Being elevated.

FIRE: Presence of God, fire of God, Holy Spirit.

GRANDPARENT: spiritual inheritance (good or evil) inheritance.

HAMMER: Word of God.

HEAD: Authority

INCENSE: Prayers

KEYS: Power

LILLIES: Beauty

LION: kingship

MIRROR: The Word of God.

These are just a few more symbols for your dreams to help you learn how to interpret them. It is my prayer that God reveal to you clearly what your purpose here for being born. It is my prayer that you develop a close or closer relationship with Him. Like I said before this is not for everyone and this is for those who want to know Him in a more intimate and different way. This book is for those who seek and will find Him. This is for those who want to walk in the blessings and not the curses of God. My prayer is that truth prevails over lies and deceit. My prayer is that the eyes of your understanding be open and enlighten.

Ephesians 1: 17-18 KJV

> *17. That the God of our Lord Jesus Christ, the Father of glory, may give unto you the spirit of wisdom and revelation in the knowledge of him.*
>
> *18. The eyes of your understanding being enlightened; that you may know what is the hope of his calling, and what the riches of the glory of his inheritance in the saints.*

If You Don't Have Dreams and Visions

Listen to me closely, if you don't have dreams and visions don't fret about that because it is not that you don't have them but you just don't remember them. Please don't let this throw you off. I have talked to many people who don't have dreams and visions, but everybody has a dream like the late Dr. Martin Luther King Jr. He had a dream that every race could come together and get alone, work together, lived together because he had a dream. You have a dream, I have a dream and we all have a dreams like owning a business, dream of being rich, and a dream vacation. We all have dreams of doing something that no one have ever done before. If you don't have dreams and remember them, please don't fret about it. God will speak to you in other ways and He speaks in many different ways. You will have to learn how He speaks to you and learn to listen for listening is a skill that must be learn. We are only here for a short time on earth but if we continually to go round and round not knowing who we are, or why we are here. When we are so unhappy with ourselves, our lifestyle, our insecurities, our weakness, and our rebellion against the creator of all. You are the apple of His eye. His plans are for you to succeed and have a good ending. I really believe that with all my heart that Jesus is the great example that He did not come to bring religion, but to have a personal one on one relationship will us. Religion will keep you bound, but a healthy relationship in Jesus gives liberty and freedom. I am not bringing you religion even though I write scriptures. These people in the bible was people who lived out God's plan for their lives that we can take notes and see the mistakes some made and avoid doing as they did. Not that if it was all bad they did, but we can learn from the good as well as the mistakes. If you don't have dreams and visions or don't remember them, you are not an outcast but you just need to find you place in the kingdom. As I said earlier we in the west coast are not familiar with what is called Kingdom, but we can learn from a biblically perspective the truth about the Kingdom. One must truly study and dig deep for understanding which is the key to understanding the Kingdom or Kingdoms.

Chapter 15

Open Heavens

An Open Heaven from My First Book

This is really the Key to all that we see in dreams and visions. At particular turning points in history, windows open and heaven is poured out upon us. God localizes His presence over the life of an individual, a church, a city or nation in outpoured blessing and power in what we often call revivals. They are special moments of time when heaven touches earth. Jesus taught this is the one true object of prayer when instructed us to ask, "your will be done on earth as it is in heaven". Which of us does not want to live under an open heaven and to revel in an unhindered experience of heaven on earth? But what does this look like and how does it actually work? In this teaching, we will first describe what an open heaven is and secondly describe how it may be experienced.

What Is an Open Heaven?

An open heaven can be described as an unhindered manifestation in the earth of all that heaven is, of God's own presence and glory. Natural laws can be temporarily or permanently suspended as heaven breaks in. Signs and wonders, miracles and healings, revelations and unusual manifestations of power begin to occur. To varying degrees' poverty, sickness, disease, and human degradation are driven back by the overpowering love of God. The most unlikely are swept into kingdom and significant wealth can flow into the church.

Generally, these seasons are characterized by at least four things: revelation, visitation, habitation, and inundation.

The Stairway to Heaven Dream

First Revelation, Jesus "read Nathaniel's mail". Saw him in the spirit; under the fig tree that He revealed his inner nature as a man without guile. Despite being stunned by this amazing revelation Jesus promised him, "You shall see greater things than that—you shall see heaven open, and the angels of God ascending and descending on the Son of Man." (John 1:50, 51KJV)

Jesus is referring to Jacob's dream of Genesis 28. Falling asleep Jacob saw a ladder resting on the earth with its top reaching into heaven-a stairway to heaven. By this means the angels of God were ascending and descending. Jesus in now the means by which heaven and earth communicate through Him. Heaven comes to earth where ministering spirits are sent to men below bearing the commands and comforts of our heavenly Father and in turn they bear the prayers and praises of the people back to heaven. In Christ, a divine interchange is now possible between heaven and earth.

Angelic visitations, dreams, visions, and prophecies are all characteristics of an open heaven. An open heaven is supernatural. Communication occurs. This is the "normal" Christian life as Paul testified, "I will go on to visions and revelations from the Lord. I know a man in Christ who fourteen years ago was caught up to the third heaven whether it was in the body or out of the body I do not know – God knows". (2 Cor. 12:2KJV) For those in Christ supernatural encounters are to be expected.

Turning Points in History

Second, visitation of an open heaven occurs during turning points in history to increase Christ's Kingdom in the earth. At the commencement of Jesus public ministry, He was baptized and as "he went up out of the water…heaven was opened, and he saw the Spirit of God descending like a dove and lighting on him and a voice from heaven said, "This is my son, whom I am welled pleased". (Matt. 3:16, 17KJV). This pattern of scripture of the Son foreshadows a moment in history when the Body of Christ and the church reaches the fullness of the stature of Christ – maturity (Ephesians 4:11-13). The heavens will increasingly open over the corporate Christ in greater seasons of divine visitation and blessings as it approaches this time.

The heavens were also opened when Stephen was killed as the first martyr / Stephen, full of the Holy Spirit, looked up to heaven and saw the glory of God, and Jesus standing at the right hand of God (Acts 7:55, 56). At this the people, Sanhedrin (religious folks), covered their ears screaming and rushed upon him, stoning him to death. Religious spirits will always resist an open heaven. But immediately, the church was scattered from Jerusalem through the persecution and the Word spread into Judea and Samaria through an open heaven as the kingdom was increased.

When it was time for the gospel to go out to the Gentiles, the heavens were again opened when Peter fell into a trance (vision) who "saw heaven opened and something like a large sheet being let down earth by its four corners" (Acts 10:9-23 KJV). Through this open-heaven revelation, the door opened to the Gentiles where Peter was shown he was not to declare unclean. What God had declared clean a whole new chapter of God's purpose for the earth began.

This generation has been called to live under an open heaven never before has the door to the Gentiles been as open as it is right now. This is the time to be pressing into God for and open-heaven revelation and outpouring –for an increase of the supernatural and therefore of Christ's kingdom in the earth.

The House of Prayer

Third, habitation began when Jacob awoke from seeing the heavens opened and a ladder with angels ascending and descending his response was, "WOW!" He said, "Surely the Lord is in this place, and I was not aware of it. He was afraid and said, "How awesome is this place! This is one other than the house of God; this is the gate of heaven…He called that place Bethel…" (Genesis 28:16-19 KJV).

When God visits, He comes to stay. He is not only interested in visitation but also habitation. He is looking for a place to dwell. Somewhere He can call home, where He can kick back and relax in a pure environment that answers to who He is. So, what creates that environment? What kind of house does He want to live in? One that's filled with Intercessory Worship. Jesus said that, "My Father's house shall be called the house of prayer".

So, an open heaven is marked by a significant increase in the spirit of prayer and of worship. No church growth program, city reaching strategy, or "anointed" entertainment will ever build the house that God lives in. He will only dwell with the humble and contrite of spirit. If we understood the implications of this, we would be on our faces. Just because we call ourselves "church" does not guarantee that we are, in fact the house of God! The Lord continues to cry out to this generation, "Heaven is my throne and earth is my footstool".

The Wealth of the Nation

Fourth, Inundation "The Lord will open the heavens, the storehouse of his bounty, to send rain on your land in season and to bless all the work of your hands. You will lend too many nations but will borrow from none the Lord will make you the head and not the tail…" (Deut 28:12, 13 KJV).

When we are living under an open heaven, not only is the Spirit outpoured bur we can often also experience increased financial blessing. While not always the case, increased spiritual outpouring can signal increased financial outpouring. It is possible though to experience the one without the other.

Despite these exceptional circumstances we can be assured from scripture that God desires to bless his children physically, spiritually, emotionally, financially etc.

In my first book, I talk a little about Open Heaven. Under an open heaven, men of God have done wonderful and great things. For there was a time when the heaven was closed, but after the cross, there is an open heaven when we pray, worship, dream, and preach.

Eli the priest: Eli was the reigning priest of the Lord at the time of Samuel's birth. Samuel had been born as a result of the cry of his barren mother's heart. Samuel's mother was named Hannah who promised God if he gave her a son, she would give him back to the Lord for his service.

God gave Hannah a son, but when Eli saw her praying and thought she was drunk, he rebuked her. Eli did not come across as a godly man and spiritual leader he could not discern the difference between godly desire and a drunkard. He was not a good family man, as he had allowed his own sons to prostitute the women of the church (1 Samuel 1-2). The only recording of God speaking to Eli is in 1st Samuel 2:27-36 where i t is a message of judgment upon him and his household for their failures to obey the commands of the Lord! It came through the Prophet. There is nothing recorded scripturally where God spoke to this priest on a personal level, or one on one. As a priest, it was Eli responsibility to mentor Samuel into the work of the ministry. History always repeat itself with the same Eli's spirit in the church where Jesus said to make disciples of men to get them ready for the work of the ministry, but the leaders or so caught up with their own personal agenda; everyone has to learn on there on through trial and error. The Word of the Lord was rare in those days and the Word of the Lord is rare now.

In 1st Samuel 3, it talks about "And the Word of the Lord was precious (rare) in those days; there was no open vision or divine revelation. "And the Lord appeared again in Shiloh: for the Lord revealed Himself to Samuel in Shiloh by the Word of the Lord." We started out with a closed heaven over the priesthood and the nation of Israel, and ends with an open heaven over the same nation. It is the same today. Just because your leader is spiritually dead, through Jesus Christ you can live under an open heaven if you seek Him with your whole heart. He is the same yesterday, today, and for ever more. This is why we should see Him where He may be found and we can live under an open heaven. This is a life style which is supernatural not natural and it is a life changing experience. This is also another way to hear the voice of God, but it also has to be developed. I love to read and now that I am older, I love to read the bible. It is the father's love letter to His people. Some of the stories are so interesting and some are actually love stories with great endings.

I learned that everything we receive from the Father comes by revelation-by hearing His voice is called "hearing the Word of the Lord." I don't want to come across religious for these people we read in the scriptures had real life experiences. When we dream and have visions, we are visited by God in night visions and He speaks in parables so we can learn to interpret how He is speaking to us. These are to be learned of Him as He continues to visit you and me to keep us on the path of righteousness. What a loving father that wants to communicate with us for he is the Creator of the Universe. In the Old Testament, the entire Prophet and some of the kings that were obedient to God operated under an open heaven. The heavens were open and the Lord gave those dreams, visions, revelation, knowledge, wisdom, and more of them was exempt for trials, error, judgment, corrections and life style of a free will so here we find the same principle applies today. If a nation is not listening to God, it lives under a closed heaven. It applies also to churches and to individual lives as a believer.

Uzziah and Isaiah: Let's Look Into The Life of These of Two

2nd Chronicles 26, we read of a very successful king by the name of Uzziah. He came to power at a young age when he was 16 years old. He allowed a spiritual man, Zechariah to impart into his life. Zechariah was a man who lived under an open heaven, because "he had understanding in the visions of God" (v. 5). That word "understanding" is a spiritual word meaning "to separate, to discern, to mark, to understand" all which depend on the power of separating, distinguishing, perceive, and vision. It means "to see or to be taught" of God in vision as the prophets. Zechariah received spiritual revelation from God and passed it on to Uzziah, so the story goes on to say Uzziah allowed pride to enter his heart that things went horribly wrong for him. He stepped outside of his realm of authority and offered incense in the temple. This was not the job of a king but the job of the Priest. In doing so Pride closed heaven over him, he came out a leper, and remained a leper until he died. The revelation of God could no longer be obeyed. It wasn't until Uzziah died that we see heaven opened again over Israel. We read about that in Isaiah 6. There are open heavens, open windows, open doors, open gates that He want to open to us all. These are what we call open heavens or open ancient portals. I want to live under an open heaven for everyone I meet. I want them to also receive the blessing of the Lord over their lives. If this scripture is true and we should test the scriptures for God is faithful to His Word.

The Mystery of the Kingdom of God

To understand dreams, visions, and the word of the kingdom of heaven which is a mystery one has to:

- **Study**: The bible says to study to show thyself approve unto God a workman may not be a shame to rightly divide the word of truth. 2 Timothy 2:15.

- **Read**: How can one study if he doesn't pick up a book and Read?

- **Comprehend**: How can one comprehend if he doesn't read and study.

- **Understand**: How can you get an understanding of what is being read if you don't study, read, comprehend, in all that getting gets an understanding.

- **Apply**: This Word is more real than anything I have ever experienced in my life, for it is the living Word that became flesh among us, and dwell among us. What are you saying? I am saying we can take the scriptures in the bible and walk in them, live them out and apply them to our everyday life. So we can say no more religion, no more tradition, no more fear, no more guessing, no more wondering if God is real and for real about His Word.

The Bible mentions 12 specific mysteries

- The Kingdom of Heaven is the mystery that Jesus refers to the most.

- The Kingdom of Heaven operates differently that the kingdoms of the world.

- Living in the Kingdom of Heaven requires us to a hidden battle with the enemy.

- Jesus has given 72 parables that compare this spiritual Kingdom with earthly matters.

- Discovering the meaning of these parables and how they apply to your life will be a battle that Jesus had-to overcome the work of Satan.

    The original intent of God was for man to have authority over the earth not over human flesh, but over the earth, but man gave away that authority when he sinned and submitted to Satan.

Jesus came to introduce His Kingdom and provide a way for man to become a citizen of it instead.

The Hebrew scribes thought the Kingdom was a political and territorial domain.

Albert Schweitzer thought the Kingdom was merely a spot in eternity, a future reality when time is stopped and a new heavenly order began.

Augustine thought it was the theocratic rule of the Church over all forms of government on earth.

"These are the thoughts and saying of the great later John Paul Jackson. For the Kingdom of Heaven is within and it manifest itself outwardly before God can advance his Kingdom in you, He has to change your heart, he has to remove the heart of stone and give you a heart of flesh. He has to impregnate your soul with the very Spirit of the Living god. This new you, this new creation, are now able to do all things through Christ who strengthens you. You're now ready to advance the Kingdom. What is the proof of this? You pray and the sick are healed. You cast out evil spirit even through prayer. You cleanse the lepers as you do these things you tell everyone around you that the Kingdom of Heaven has come near them."

Chapter 16
The Living Word and Stars

The Lords' Prayer

> *Our Father which art in heaven, Hallowed be they name Thy kingdom come. Thy will be done in earth as it is in heaven. Give us this day our daily bread. And forgive us our debts, as we forgive our debtors, and lead us not into temptation, but deliver us from evil: for thine are the kingdom, and power and the glory, forever. Amen (Matthew 6:9-13 KJV).*

Even in the Lords' Prayer, Thy Kingdom come was a prayer that the Kingdom of God will come in the earth as his Kingdom is in heaven. The mysteries of the Kingdom will be revealed to which God wants to reveal them to in these last days.

Baby Dreams

Let us do one of the most common dreams and this one is when we dream of being pregnant or having a baby that is already born. Remember dreams are very symbolic and not so literally.
Dreaming of being pregnant speaks of a ministry, a business venture, or a Destiny (your destiny).

Now if the baby is already born then God has birthed something through you. It is already shaped, but need to be developed and matured. If your baby has on blue colors, blue is the color for revelation. Your entire ministry has to be developed and matured. I had a baby dream that I birthed a baby boy and he had on the colors blue. I am to take care of this ministry that the Lord has entrusted me with for He gives me much revelation in this. So you ask what this ministry that He has given you is. I am glad you asked for my ministry is writing books about the Mystery of the Kingdom. I am taking it one step at a time for I don't know what else he has in store for me for I am walking by faith and not by sight.

There are mysteries that only you can discovery. You and only you have been called to dispatch these Mysteries of the Kingdom to the Body of Christ and to a dying world. This will be your purpose, your call, and your destiny for which you were born, but you have to seek it out. You have to find out your own purpose for being born.

- Ask God to give you a Bible verse to deal with the specific situation you dealing with.

- Ask God to tell you a song you may hear on the Radio.

- Ask God to show you people who can use an encouraging word for you.

- Ask God to help you find your purpose and give you to meet the people that are purpose to help you on your journey.

- Ask God for confirmation, preparation, and proclamation.

If you are sincere and sick and tired of the same old, you. God will see your heart and reveal things about yourself you didn't know. Our minds are the battleground. Our spirits are complete if we are saved and a new creature in Christ. There is a purpose for being born into this earth realm. It is now time to find out what is our call and purpose for being here. We must study the Word of God daily or as much as we can to find out what and who we are called to do. Only the creator can tell you and I what our purpose for being born and coming to the earth. When the Word of God is preached or we study His Word, then knowledge is imparted to the spirit and our spirit begins to bear witness with the spirit of truth. This becomes revelation knowledge so we are to receive the Word and then meditate on the Word of God. I love this for it is the Word of God that we can apply to our everyday life situation for His Word is alive.

***Hebrews 4:12-13 KJV** For the Word of God is quick, and powerful, and sharper than any two-edged sword, piercing even to the dividing asunder of soul and spirit, and of the joints and marrow, and is a discerner of the thoughts and intents of the heart. 13. Neither is there any creature that is not manifest in his sight: but all things are naked and opened unto the eyes of him with whom we have to do.*

The Living Word

The living Word lives on the inside of you to help you through this journey in life. The Word came in the form of human to be an example to the people who have received Him into their heart. The living Word testifies of Jesus Christ from Genesis to Revelation. The living Word makes men wise unto salvation. It reveals to us God's ways unto salvation and not mans' ways for He has chosen the foolish things of the world to confound the wise. Through the living Word we are regenerated for the living Word is a seed. We are to produce seed after its' own kind so to be regenerated is to be reborn are born again with the life of God inside which is the living Word. As newborn babies in Christ we should desire the milk of the Word. The living Word is the milk that causes us to grow in our spiritual life it is of the most importance to daily come to the Lord in his Word, and drink the spiritual milk. The living Word is also bread of life.

***Matthew4:4 KJV** Man shall not live by bread alone, but by every that proceeds out of the mouth of God.*

The living Word is not just milk, but also the bread of life so we can grow from needing to eat the Lord's Word every day, just as we can grow from needing to eat our physical meals each day. Jesus was living as a man in the flesh needing daily natural food to survive in the natural but also took God's Word as His spiritual bead. If Jesus is our example to the narrow way, then we are in good company looking unto Jesus who is the author and finisher of our faith. The Living Word makes us complete because all scriptures are God breathed and profitable for teaching, for conviction, for correction, for instruction in righteousness, that the man of God may be complete, fully equipped for every good work. (2 Timothy 3:16-17)

What this Living Word Mean for Us?

Every day, we can continue in and profit from God's Word. We can pray His will, His purpose, and His call in our life. We can apply this living Word to every situation in our life for it is alive in us and will do whatever it needs to do to accomplish the purpose and the call. The Word of God is life application for our life so we can take every Word and apply it to our own life. The Living Word of God is very much alive as we learn to live it, walk it, and work out our own soul salvation. This living word will totally set you free if we abide in His Word and His Word abide in us for it is living and active.

Hebrew 4:12 KJV For the Word of God is quick alive and sharper than a two-edged sword, it penetrates to divide soul, and spirit, and joints, and marrow; it judges the thoughts and attitude of the heart.

God's Word will produce fruits in you. So in order for the living Word to work and produce fruit in your life, we must read, study, and meditate on His Word day and night by making it a living extension of your life. Then that it can produce spiritual fruit in you for "all scripture is given by inspiration of God, and is profitable for doctrine, for reproof, for correction, for instruction in righteousness." (2 Timothy 3:16 KJV)

Put your faith and trust in the Lord Jesus Christ who is the Living Word and your Lord and Savior of the world for He was in the beginning and He is the Living Word. Once we know about the Word, then we will find ourselves living the Active Word because the Word is now alive in us. Then our focus is to apply what we know and have learned as we study the Word or Scriptures. The Holy Spirit will show us h o w t o apply the Word to our life, situations and circumstances. This is awesome that the

Living Word of God is among us so not only we will have to not only talk it but we will have to walk and live it out.

You Are A Star

You are a star and this is why the enemy hates you. His purpose is to keep you from being all God destined you to become. The enemy steals our stars, dreams, visions, purpose, and destiny, for we are destined for greatness. Before we were born, as soon as your mother conceived you in the womb, the enemy begin his tracking of destruction assignment against you.

Revelation 12:1 KJV
And there appeared a great wonder in heaven; a woman cloth with the sun and moon under her feet, and upon her head a crown of twelve stars. 2. She being with child cried travailing in birth and pain to be delivered.

The stars represent the twelve tribes of Israel and these stars upon her head of the woman represent the people of God. For God call His people, his wife for she is crying and travailing in birth pain to bring forth the stars. We are all born into this world with a star to bring the Kingdom of God back into alignment. Our dreams, visions, purpose, gifts, talents, and destiny all play a part of our star. The enemy is there at birth to stop the plan and purpose of God in your life. Soon as Jesus was born, the devil used King Herod to order a hit on the baby Jesus. His orders were to kill all males that were born two years old and under in order to stop the destiny of The Messiah.

> *Matthew2:7 KJV Then Herod when had privily called the wise men, inquired of them diligently what time the star appeared. 8. And he sent them to Bethlehem and said, God and search diligently for the young child; and when you have found him bring me word again, that I may come and worship him also. 9. When they had*

> *heard the King they departed; and lo, the star, which they saw in the east, went before them till it came and stood over where the young child was. 10. and when they saw the star, they rejoice with exceedingly great joy.*

In my study of the stars, I found twenty-one things the Devil wants to stop your star from shining in your life.

1. **Your Purpose**: It is purpose that gives life definition and meaning. A life with no purpose becomes worthless.

2. **Your Destiny:** The Word of God says the desires of our hearts shall be granted, but when destiny is killed, frustration sets in

3. **Your Vision:** Vision takes a person to their destination and vision creates room for the next level and enlarge your coast. When vision is killed, stagnancy prevails.

4. **Your Gifts:** The gifts of a man shall make room for him, and cause him to stand before great men says the Word of God.

5. **The Fruit of your Body:** The devil's desire for your children and children children's to be destroyed. He is after your generation and its non-existence to come to pass.

6. **The Fruit of Your Labor:** The greatest delight of the enemy is profitless hard work. He delights in men and women not having anything to show for their labor.

7. **Your Marriage:** Marriages crash daily at an all time high rate. Once family unity is broken, the society and nation will have a problem with unity.

8. **Your Calling:** The enemy doesn't want you to fulfill your ministry.

9. **Your Potential:** This is what you can do but have not done yet, for you have the potential to do it.

10. **The Instrument of Blessing:** When the devil takes this away you will not have test money.

11. **Your Expression:** This is your lack of faith.

12. **Your Star:** Shining Star Signifies a colorful destiny. When the devil steals and kills your star, the light will go out and the end result is a wasted and unfulfilled life. 13. Your Voice: Everyone has been given a voice by God but the devil wants to silence your voice.

14. **Your Life:** This represents your divine assignment in life.

15. **Your divine helper:** Those God has risen up to assist you and the devil's job is to make sure you miss your divine help.

16. **Your Career:** This is what you are able to do. When you career is under attack, it will struggle to succeed.

17. **Your Name:** The devil enjoys erasing your name from existence.

18. **Your Destiny:** Destiny is summoned up as your mission here on earth.

19. **The Promise of God:** When the devil attacks the promises of God has for you, they will not come to pass your life.

20. **Your Future:** As believer our future is heaven.

21. **Your Present Life:** The enemy does not want anyone to complete their divine number of days on earth.

John 10:10 KJV I have come that you may have life and have it more abundantly.

You are a star and have a star so Satan wants to be above the stars of God, because he wants your star (worship).

> ***Isaiah 14:13-14 KJV***
> ***"You said in your heart, "I will ascend to Heaven; I***

will raise my throne above the stars of God, and I will sit on the Mount of the assembly in the recesses of the north, I will ascend above the heights of the clouds; I will make myself like the Most High."

When you worship, the devil tries to steal your star so it not shines. It is your time to shine now so that you know the truth and it shall set you free. Jesus came to set the captives free from the enemy of your soul and self- destruction. It is that feeling inside of you that is always speaking to you in your dreams, visions, and purpose letting you know that you are a shining star. In dreams and visions, the stars speak of the nation of Israel and generations. The sun speaks of glory, brightness, and light in Christ. The moon symbolizes light in darkness, and signs of the Son of Man, Jesus.

You Are Here to Make an Impact

You are here to make an impact in this world and with all that is going on. You are here to make a difference so find your place in the earth and let your star shine. Do not give up on your dreams and visions that God has placed inside of you for the enemy will try to sidetrack and stop you from completing your assignment in the earth. It may be delayed, but never denied so come on child of God let your STAR SHINE! I pray that I have made an impact on the person that is reading this book. My prayer for you is to not give up after all you have been through and take you experiences to use for positive energy to help somebody else. Yes, you have been though the fire and the flood, but thank God you are still here to make your impact. It is not too late in life even when there are many obstacles and challenges to face; if we just believe in the Creator of everything going to the source to find out our place in the world to make a difference and change for betterment of generations to come.

George Washington Carver Agricultural Chemist

Born in 1864 at Diamond Grove, Mo; educated at Simpson college and Iowa State College: on staff of Iowa State College 1894-1896; of Tuskegee Institute from 1896; elected fellow in Royal Society of Arts (London), 1916; Spingarn Medal. 1923; Roosevelt Medal, 1939 honorary degrees in 1928 and 1941; developed 300 products from the peanut, 125 from sweet potato, and 75 from pecan; died in 1943.

"Nothing is more beautiful than the loveliness of the woods before sunrise. At no other time have I so sharp an understanding of what God means to do with me as in these hours of dawn. When other folk are asleep, I hear God best."

I discover nothing in my laboratory. If I come here of myself I am lost. But I can do all things through Christ. I am God's servant. His agent, for here God and I are alone. I am just the instrument through which He speaks, and I would be able to do more if I were to stay in closer touch with him. With my prayers I mix my labors, and sometimes god is pleased to bless the results."

I indulge in very little lip service, but ask the Great Creator silently, daily, and often many times a day, to permit me to speak to Him through the three great kingdoms of the world which He has created-----the animal, mineral, and vegetable kingdom-----to understand their relations to each other, and our relations to each other, and our relations to them and to the great God who made all of us. I ask Him daily and often momentarily to give me wisdom, understanding and bodily strength to do His will; hence I am asking and receiving all the time.